FOCUS ON · WELSH HISTORY

Wales

AND

Britain

in the Early
Modern World

c1500 – c1760

Roger Turvey

Hodder & Stoughton

A MEMBER OF THE HODDER HEADLINE GROUP

Acknowledgments

The cover illustration is a portrait of Sir John Perrot, reproduced by kind permission of a private collection/the sixth Baron of Hampton.

National Portrait Gallery 4a, 10c, 14c, 15, 16a, 18a, 19f, 21d, 25f, 42c, 46a, 57d, 67d, 79f; National Museum of Wales 6b, 20c, 64d; Mansell Collection 7c, 22e, 31j, 40b, 49e, 53a, 70b; The Royal Collection ©. Her Majesty the Queen 12b, 47b, 48d; Reproduced by permission of Viscount De L'Isle, from his private collection 12d; Private collection/Bridgeman Art Library, London 13e; Private Collection/Sherborne Castle 13h; Cadw: Welsh Historic Monuments. Crown Copyright 17h; Cadw: Welsh Historic Monuments. Crown Copyright/Alan Sorrell 17l, 28c; Sir George Godber in *Medieval Wall Paintings* 18b; Reproduced by permission of the Royal Mail 22a; British Library (C33a8), (C33a19), (E378[6]) and (E89[3]), (E541[21]), (E684[1]) - 23f, 51d, 51e, 55c, 56b; National Library of Wales 23g, 38b, 39d, 45f, 59, 62b, 64a, 72b, 74c, 75f; Beaver Photography 26a; Crown Copyright. Royal Commission on the Ancient and Historical Monuments of Wales. 26c, 64c; College of Arms, London (MS. M6, f.41v) 27d; Private Collection/The Duke of Northumberland 27e; Staatliche Gemalde-Galerie, Berlin/Bridgeman Art Library 28b; The National Trust 29f; The Fotomas Index 30a, 71g (flea); New York Metropolitan Museum of Art 32b; Trustees of the National Library of Scotland 34a; National Maritime Museum 35a, 36c, 37f, 37j; Ron Avent/Gwasg Carreg Gwalch 39e; Culver Pictures, New York 40c; Mary Evans Picture Library 41d; Robin Price/Geraint Wyn Jones 44b; Hulton Deutsch Collection 49f, 58a, 76b; Private Collection/Lord Tollemarche 54a; By permission of the Earl of Rosebery on loan to the Scottish National Portrait Gallery 55b; Weidenfeld and Nicolson Limited 56a; City Hall, Cardiff 60b; Reproduced by kind permission of the Principal, Fellows and Scholars of Jesus College, Oxford 61c; British Museum 61f, 75g; Wilton House Trust 62a; St. Bride Printing Library 63g; Christ's Hospital, Horsham, West Sussex 66b; Museum of London 66c; University of Reading, Rural History Centre 68a; Metropolitan Museum of Art, the Elisha Whittelsey Fund 69g; Bibliotèque Nationale 70a; Royal College of Physicians/Bridgeman Art Library 70d; Istituto e Museo di Storia della Scienza, Firenze 71f; Michael Holford 71g (microscope); Museum of Welsh Folk Life 72a, 72c, 78b; E.T. Archive 29d, 77c; Westair Reproductions Limited/Marian Delyth 78c; Reproduced by permission of the Marquess of Bath, Longleat House, Warminster, Wiltshire 79d; Yale Center for British Art 79e.

Every effort has been made to trace and acknowledge ownership of copyright. The Publishers will be glad to make suitable arrangements with any copyright holders whom it has not been possible to contact.

British Library Cataloguing in Publication Data

A catalogue for this title is available from the British Library

ISBN   0 340 64348 X

First Published 1995
Impression number   10 9 8 7 6 5 4 3 2 1
Year   1999 1998 1997 1996 1995

This book is published with the financial support of the Curriculum and Assessment Authority for Wales.

Typeset by The University of Wales, Aberystwyth, Wales
Printed in Great Britain for Hodder & Stoughton Educational, a division of Hodder Headline Plc, 338 Euston Road, London NW1 3BH by Cambridge University Press, Cambridge

Contents

A Welshman becomes King of England

A Portrait of Henry Tudor 20 years after Bosworth (1505)

B Henry Tudor's march through Wales

Richard III became king of England in 1483 after the rightful king, Edward V, disappeared. Richard made many enemies and became very unpopular because of his cruelty. Many people thought he had murdered his young nephew Edward.

Richard was a member of the Yorkist family that had taken the Crown from their enemies the Lancastrians. The Lancastrians decided this was the best time to try to take back the throne. There was a problem. After 30 years of war they had nobody left alive who had a direct claim to the throne. So they looked around for a suitable candidate and found Henry **Tudor**.

Henry Tudor seemed an unlikely choice for king. He was born in Wales, son of a 14-year-old widow and had probably never been to England. He was young, poor, inexperienced and few people had heard of him. He had been living in France for 14 years to escape the Yorkists. Despite this, in August 1485, he led the last successful invasion of England and Wales.

Henry landed in the county and country of his birth, Pembrokeshire in Wales. Milford Haven provided a safe harbour for his ships. It was far enough away from Richard's army in England. His uncle Jasper had been Earl of Pembroke so he had many friends there.

Henry realised that his army of 2,000 foreign **mercenaries** was too small to defeat Richard but he hoped to increase it by recruiting in Wales. He believed that, as a Welshman, he could appeal to the people of Wales for help. Henry was better known in Wales than in England. This was because an important group of Welsh people, the **bards** and poets, travelled the country singing his praises. The poets were respected and their poems and songs were very popular. They sang songs about the *Mab Darogan* (Son of Prophecy). He was said to be the Welshman that would one day sit upon the English throne. Henry was to fulfil that **prophecy.**

However, Henry knew that to be successful he had to attract the support of the **gentry.** They were rich and powerful landowners who

The British [Welsh] people would occupy the island again at some time in the future, once the appointed moment should come.

C This prophecy was written by Geoffrey of Monmouth in 1135. It appeared in his well-known book *History of the Kings of Britain*

> Summon the Welsh to thy side and they will come to thee; demand England under thee and the despoiling [destruction] of her people.

D   This was written by a Welsh poet to Henry Tudor

ruled in the country. They could bring men and money to help his cause. But they also had the power to stop him. Henry's luck held. The most important landowner in Wales, Rhys ap Thomas of Dinefwr, joined him at Welshpool. He hoped Henry would reward him if he helped Henry achieve his aims.

On the week-long march through Wales nearly 3,000 Welshmen joined the Lancastrian army. Henry's Welsh-speaking grandfather, Owen Tudor, had originally come from Anglesey, and because of this many supporters came from north Wales. But the largest number came from Carmarthen in south Wales under the command of Rhys ap Thomas. Thanks to his fellow countrymen, Henry's army doubled in size.

On 22 August 1485 the Yorkists under Richard III and the Lancastrians under Henry Tudor met in battle at Bosworth field. Henry's army was outnumbered two to one, but his Welsh soldiers fought bravely until they were helped by an English family: the Stanleys. The Stanleys' army tipped the balance in Henry's favour.

Richard fought with great courage but he was killed by a Welshman; Rhys ap Maredudd. Rhys was one of Henry's most loyal knights who carried his banner during the battle - *Y Ddraig Goch* (The Red Dragon). Today it is the National Flag of Wales.

Henry owed Wales and the Welsh a great debt. Without them he may not have become king and the Tudor **dynasty** may not have come to rule England and Wales.

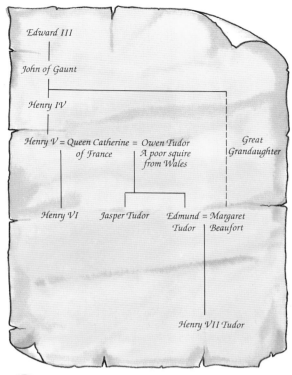

E   The Tudor family tree

> The Welsh may now be said to have recovered their former independence, for the most wise and fortunate Henry VII is a Welshman.

F   This was written by an ambassador from Venice who was visiting England in 1486

---

1 Put these events in the order in which they happened:
  a) Henry Tudor lands in Wales;
  b) Richard III becomes king;
  c) Henry Tudor goes to live in France;
  d) the Battle of Bosworth.

2 Look at source E.
How could Henry claim the throne through his father?

3 Look at source B.
  a) How long did Henry take to march through Wales?
  b) The distance between Dale and Shrewsbury is 180 miles. What was the average distance Henry and his army marched every day?

c) How could this have affected Henry's chances of winning at Bosworth field?

4 Read sources C, D, and F.
  a) Which of the sources do you think shows that the Welsh hated the English? Give a reason for your answer.
  b) For each source write down whether it is primary or secondary. Give a reason in each case for your choice.

5 Working in pairs, think about the question 'Why did the Welsh people help Henry Tudor to become king?'
  a) List each reason on a separate line.
  b) For each reason give a mark out of ten to show how important you think it was to the Welsh people.

2 *T*owards a United Kingdom

A   Wales and England in 1500

Key:
- Population over 10 000
- Population between 5 000 and 10 000
- Population between 2 000 and 4 000

SCOTLAND

Newcastle

York

Lincoln

Wrexham

Shrewsbury

Norwich

King's Lynn
Bury St. Edmunds

Yarmouth

Worcester
Coventry
Lavenham
Ipswich

WALES
Hereford
Colchester

Haverfordwest
Carmarthen
Gloucester

LONDON
Bristol
Reading
Canterbury

Salisbury

Exeter

0   50   100   150   200

Kilometres

If you had travelled with Henry Tudor through Wales and England in August 1485 what would you have seen? Henry must have noticed how poor the land and people of Wales were when compared to England. Wales was a small country with a population of about 275,000. This is the population of Cardiff today. England had a population of 2.75 million, ten times that of Wales. England was also five times bigger than Wales.

Henry must also have noticed the differences between the people of Wales and England. Almost all of the people of Wales spoke Welsh. Few of them could understand English. Those that could were usually wealthy landowners who wished to serve the kings of England. English people who came to live in Wales did not bother to learn Welsh. They thought it was a strange language spoken by a strange people. The English did not understand Welsh customs or the culture of the people. They did not trust the Welsh.

Henry spent a week marching through Wales on his way to Bosworth, but once he became king he was never to return. Marching through Wales would have been difficult. It was a land of high mountains, deep river valleys and vast forests. There were few roads and even fewer bridges over wide rivers like the Tywi or Conwy.

There were few towns in Wales. The largest were Carmarthen, Haverfordwest and Brecon in the south and Wrexham in the north. They had populations of around 2,000 but most towns were much smaller than that. They were important because they were trading centres where weekly markets were held. Nine out of ten people in Wales and England lived in small villages scattered around the countryside. Most of the villages in England had a population of less than a 100. In Wales they were even smaller.

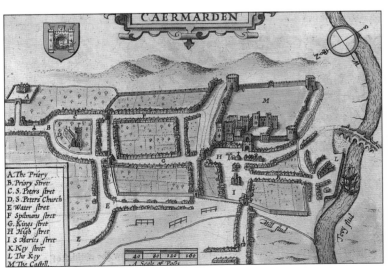

CAERMARDEN

A The Priory
B. Priory Street
C. S. Peters street
D. S. Peters Church
E Water street
F Spilmans street
G. Kings street
H. High street
I S Maries street
K Key street
L The Key
M The Castell.

40   80   120   160

A Scale of Pases

B   A plan of Carmarthen by John Speed (1611). This was the largest town in Wales

C A contemporary view of London (1620)

The largest and most important building in these villages was the church. People took their religion seriously. They attended church regularly. They believed in God and respected the village priest.

Almost all of the people lived and worked on the land. They were farmers. A few owned their own farms, some rented small plots of land but most worked for rich and powerful landowners. They lived on what they could grow, but life was tough and the work hard. Most struggled to feed the family.

Unlike England, the soil in much of Wales is poor so it is not a good place to grow crops. Only on the island of Anglesey and the lowlands of Pembrokeshire and Glamorgan would you have seen large open fields of wheat and barley. These were a common sight in southern England.

Most farmers in Wales and the north of England used their land to graze cattle and sheep. Cattle were needed to feed the growing populations of the large English towns like London and Bristol. Wool was needed to make cloth and the demand for cloth was growing. Although cloth making became England's most important industry there were others. There was tin mining in Cornwall, lead mining in Derbyshire and iron mining in Kent. In Wales the coal industry was small but growing. Lead and silver were being mined in Cardiganshire and copper in Anglesey.

London is a stinking city, the filthiest in all of the world.

D Sir Philip Hoby's description of London (1578). He was an Englishman who had travelled in Europe

[London] abounds with every article of luxury, as well as with the necessaries of life. But the most remarkable thing in London [are] the shops.

E An Italian visitor's description of London (1500)

The English are … cunning, treacherous, and thieves; above 300 are said to be hanged annually in London.

F Paul Hentzner, a German visitor to England describes the English: *Travels in England* (1593)

---

1 Read the text and sources.
 a) Make a list of the differences between Wales and England at the beginning of the Tudor period.
 b) Which, in your opinion, was the biggest difference? Say why.
 c) Compare the Wales that Henry Tudor knew with the Wales that you know today. Write a paragraph describing the similarities and differences.

2 Read and look at sources A to F.
 a) In your opinion, why might Welsh people wish to live in a city like London?
 b) Give two reasons why some Londoners might not have liked living there.
 c) Explain why you think Sir Philip Hoby's opinion of London was so different from that of the Italian visitor.

A Tudor Wales: before and after union

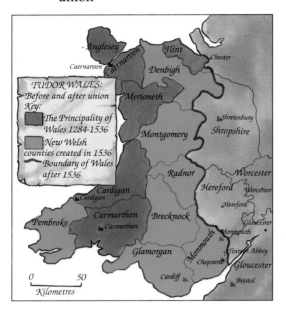

For or against union?

Here are the views of some modern historians.

Wales was 'Englished' in law and structure, and was generally content [happy] to be so for the advantages [union] provided.

B G R Elton: *Reform and Reformation* (1977)

As a positive English effort to destroy the nation's civilisation, London's policy was to destroy the language.

C In his book, *Land of My Fathers* (1974), Gwynfor Evans describes the union

It [union] gave Wales a better order than she had enjoyed for years and at the same time provided opportunities to the Welsh gentry both in England and in Wales itself.

D J D Mackie: *The Earlier Tudors* (1952)

The union of Wales and England

Between 1282 and 1543 Wales lost her independence. In 1282 Edward I killed Llywelyn, the last of the great Welsh princes, and conquered the whole country. At Rhuddlan in 1284 he passed a statute (law) which divided the country into two different areas. Edward took control of all of Llywelyn's lands and made his eldest son Prince of Wales. This land was known as the Principality and was ruled by the king's English officials.

The rest of the country was ruled by great lords who had conquered much of Wales before 1283. These lands were known as the Marches of Wales and were ruled by English Marcher Lords. They treated their lands as private property and sometimes they took no notice of the king's orders. They kept private armies, had their own laws and they often bullied their Welsh tenants.

Henry Tudor's victory at Bosworth in 1485 made the Welsh very happy. Those who lived in the Marches thought Henry would free them from the harsh and unfair rule of the Marcher Lords. They were to be disappointed. The new king was too busy in England keeping his throne safe from his enemies. He did not want to upset the Marcher Lords in case they **rebelled.**

Welsh people who lived in the Principality had better luck. Because the king owned these lands he was able to reward those Welsh leaders who had helped him become king. They were given titles and important jobs. Sir Rhys ap Thomas was given power in the south and William Gruffydd in the north.

When Henry VIII was king he became concerned with reports of lawlessness and disorder in the Marcher lands. The Marcher Lords were blamed for an increase in crimes like cattle stealing, robbery

Ambitious Welsh gentlemen queue for jobs

and murder. Some criminals were breaking the law in England and escaping to Wales where they were given employment by these lords. The king's law officers were afraid to arrest them. Henry VIII believed that the Marcher Lords were becoming too powerful and might rebel against him.

Henry VIII was especially worried because many people did not like the changes he was making in the Church. (See Chapter 4). They might ask his enemies, the kings of France and Spain, to invade England through Wales. Henry never forgot that his father had done just that in 1485 and it could happen again.

In 1534 the king chose Rowland Lee for the job of ruling Wales. He was given the power to hang criminals, punish Marcher Lords and defend the coast of Wales from invasion. Lee was a cruel man. He once hanged a dead criminal to show people that no one could escape his justice. Lee was feared and hated by almost everyone. But his hard work brought greater law and order to Wales.

Lee's work prepared the way for Henry VIII's main plan for Wales: union with England. The king wanted to get rid of the Marcher Lords and take control of the whole of Wales. He thought this would make him more powerful. In 1536 and 1543 the king passed laws which changed Wales forever. The laws abolished (got rid of) the Marcher Lordships. The Marches and Principality were united and, like England, the whole country was divided into counties; 13 in Wales. The Welsh were given the same rights as the English. They could become Members of Parliament and hold important offices like Justice of the Peace (JP) or sheriff. These laws made it easier for Henry VIII to rule Wales.

The people of Wales were pleased to be free of the Marcher Lords. But some people were unhappy. They said the union of Wales with England was not good for Welsh culture. English law replaced Welsh law. English became the language of the law courts. Welsh people who wanted to become JPs, MPs and sheriffs had to speak English. The rich and powerful landowners of Wales were behaving more like the English and they eventually began to ignore the Welsh language. Despite this, the language and culture of Wales managed to survive.

Some Welsh people did very well out of the Union. In Caernarvon, Denbigh and Radnor, many Welsh landowners were able to buy land, cattle and buildings from Henry. Many of these landowners became Members of Parliament of their counties or Justices of the Peace.

 E Simon Mason: *The Making of the UK (1992)* - a school textbook

No Welsh thief will get the better of me!

 F Rowland Lee is said to have hanged 5,000 criminals in 9 years

---

1 **What part did these people play in uniting Wales and England:**
   a) **Edward I;**
   b) **Henry VII;**
   c) **Rowland Lee;**
   d) **Henry VIII?**
   e) **Which person in this list is the odd one out? Give a reason for your choice.**

2 **Read sources B, C, D, and E.**
   a) **Which do you think was written by a Welshman? Explain how you decided.**

b) **Which Welsh people benefited from the union and which did not?**

3 **Read the text and sources carefully.**
   a) **Make a list of the causes of the union of Wales and England.**
   b) **State briefly the terms of the laws of 1536 and 1543.**
   c) **Note briefly some of the consequences of the union on Welsh culture.**

How did Tudor monarchs use their power?

Between 1485 and 1603 five members of the Tudor family became kings and queens of Wales and England. All **monarchs** believed they had been chosen by God to rule their kingdom. This idea was known as **Divine Right.** Each new monarch took part in a ceremony called a **Coronation.** During this ceremony the monarch promised to rule wisely and fairly, to protect the realm and its people and to ensure prosperity. In return the monarch's most important **subjects** swore an oath of allegiance in which they promised to be loyal to the new king or queen.

Everything favours the king, especially an immense treasure and because all the nobles of the realm know the royal wisdom and fear him or bear him extraordinary affection. England has never been so [peaceful] and obedient as at present.

 A   This was written by the Ambassador from Milan, Italy (1497)

His mind was brave and resolute and never, even in moments of great danger, deserted him. In government he was shrewd and prudent so that no-one dared to get the better of him through deceit or guile. He was gracious, kind [and] his hospitality was splendidly generous ... He gradually stopped being fair and sank into a state of greed. All of his subjects who were wealthy when found guilty of any fault were ... fined ... to gain their fortunes.

D   Polydore Vergil was an Italian from Venice who settled in England. He was employed at the Courts of Henry VII and Henry VIII. This extract is taken from his book *Anglica Historia* (The History of England) (1512)

With all Christian princes he made alliances.
His might was feared everywhere, both inside and outside his kingdom.
By the people he was obeyed as much as any other king.
For many a day his land lived in peace and quiet.
During times of danger he calculated [thought] in a cold and clever way.
He got [news] of any treason plotted against him.
Immense were his treasures and riches, and fair his buildings in the latest style.

B   Extract from Bishop Fisher's sermon at Henry VII's funeral (1509)

C   *(right)* Painting of Queen Elizabeth I at her coronation (1559)

The symbols of power at a coronation. The Archbishop of Canterbury led the ceremony and anointed the monarch with holy oil

Coronation throne with canopy

The Coronation Crown

TUDOR MONARCHS

Royal Sceptres which stand for power and justice ~ the dove mercy

Rich robes edged in ermine stand for wealth

Bracelets stand for sincerity and wisdom

The orb stands for the world under the power of Christ

The jewelled sword is for the monarch to guard their subjects

The golden spurs stand for Knighthood

Henry is so greedy that all the riches in the world would not satisfy him … [The king] does not trust a single man … and will not cease to dip his hand in blood as long as he doubts the people.

 This was written by the French Ambassador to the king of France (1540)

It is certain that Henry made no distinction [difference] between himself as a person and himself as a king. To him they were one and the same thing. He was a 24 hour-a-day monarch, for he had no private life that existed outside his [kingship] … being king was not to be worked at … as it had been for his father … it was a natural state of affairs … that required no effort and no particular training.

G K Randell: *Henry VIII and the Government of England* (1991)

The young king [Henry VIII] had brilliance but his talents were ill disciplined … He attended to the business of government only … when the mood took him and when the pursuit of pleasure allowed it. He found the act of writing 'tedious [boring] and painful'… He made a slight illness a ready excuse for refusing to work for days on end. Affairs of state might be shelved in favour of … his 'harts and hounds'.

H C Morris: *The Tudors* (1955)

1 **Using source E, make a list of which symbols at the coronation showed that the monarch was:**
   a) wealthy;
   b) powerful and just;
   c) a supporter of the Church
   d) a protector of their subjects;
   e) a brave soldier;
   f) wise?

2 **Read sources A, B and D. Divide your page into two columns headed 'strengths' and 'weaknesses'.**
   a) Now find and list the strengths and weaknesses of Henry Tudor as king.
   b) Which of the three sources is the most and which is least reliable? Explain your choice.

3 **Read sources F, G and H.**
   a) What do you learn about Henry VIII from source F?
   b) What does the writer of source H consider to have been Henry VIII's weaknesses?
   c) How does source H disagree with source G? Explain why modern historians sometimes differ in their views of Henry VIII.

4 **Compare Henry VII with Henry VIII. Who do you think was the better king? Explain your choice.**

A   An order issued by Sir William Cecil, Elizabeth's chief minister, in 1570

> No one's mind is quicker than hers, no memory more retentive ... French and Italian she speaks like English; [she speaks] Latin with fluency.

C   Roger Ascham, Elizabeth's tutor (1550)

D   (below) Contemporary painting of the Court. Elizabeth is shown dancing with her favourite Robert Dudley, the Earl of Leicester. [Unknown artist]

Elizabeth I (1558-1603): a case study

The Tudors were the first monarchs to employ artists to paint portraits of the royal family. A portrait was a way of showing a monarch's subjects what the monarch looked like. However, many portraits were copied from one original. Portraits were like photographs but with one difference; they were painted to create an image which would impress the ordinary people. Elizabeth banned paintings showing her to be ugly, old or weak. Portraits did not just represent the person. They often contained other information on the power and achievements of that monarch.

B   Portrait of Elizabeth as a 14-year-old princess (about 1547). [Unknown artist]

On her head she wore a great reddish coloured wig … As for her face it is very aged. Her teeth are very yellow and irregular … Many of them are missing, so that one cannot understand her easily when she speaks.

F Report on Elizabeth sent by the French Ambassador to the King of France (1595)

Her face was oblong, fair but wrinkled; her eyes small, yet black and pleasant; her nose a little hooked, her lips narrow … her hair … an auburn colour, but false.

G Paul Hentzner, a German visitor, met Elizabeth in 1598

H Elizabeth in procession (1600). [Attributed to Robert Peake]

E *(above)* The Armada Portrait (1588). [George Gower]

1 a) **Using sources B, D, E, F, G, and H, write a paragraph describing what Elizabeth I looked like at different times in her life.**
   b) **Look at source B. Why might this portrait of Elizabeth be more useful than the other paintings as evidence of what she looked like?**
   c) **Explain why it is so difficult to find out exactly what Elizabeth I looked like.**

2 a) **Which of the sources suggest that Elizabeth was an intelligent person?**
   b) **Look at source D. What does this painting reveal about Elizabeth's character?**
   c) **Look at source E. Study the painting closely. What image does it give of Elizabeth?**

3 a) **Look at Source H. How has the artist made Elizabeth look powerful and the most important person in the painting?**
   b) **Which of the written sources would you choose to support your answer to the previous question? Explain why you chose it.**

4 Henry VIII and the Roman Catholic Church

The greatest changes in Europe during the sixteenth century were religious changes. In 1500 there was only one Church and all Christians were members of it. It was called the Catholic Church and its leader was the Pope who lived in Rome. But by 1600 there were two Christian Churches, Roman Catholic and **Protestant.** Although people still believed in the same God they disagreed on how best to worship Him. This disagreement led to violence in some countries and wars between others.

These religious changes began in Germany in 1517 when a monk called Martin Luther criticised the Catholic Church and the Pope. He thought they had become too wealthy, powerful and, worst of all, corrupt. Luther wanted to reform (change) the Church but the Pope would not listen. Many people agreed with Luther, and his ideas began to spread all over Europe. The Pope **excommunicated** him and his followers.

Henry VIII did not like Luther's protest against the Pope. Like his Welsh and English subjects, Henry was a Catholic. In 1521 he wrote a book supporting the Pope. As a reward the Pope gave him the title *Fidei Defensor* or Defender of the Faith.

Henry also attacked Luther's Protestant ideas because he feared that criticism of the Church might encourage people to criticise the monarchy. This had happened to some of the Princes in Germany. To stop this happening in his kingdom, Henry set about **persecuting** all Protestants. The Pope supported him.

By 1534 Henry, like Luther, had quarrelled with the Pope. Henry's opinions about the power of the Pope and the wealth of the Church had changed. Why?

The man responsible for changing the king's opinion of the Church and the Pope was his chief minister Thomas Cromwell. Cromwell convinced the king that he should declare himself Head of the Church in Wales and England instead of the Pope. Henry knew that to do this he needed the support of the leading people in the kingdom and in the Church.

The most important man in the Church, Thomas Cranmer the Archbishop of Canterbury, supported the king's plan. Cromwell got Parliament to support Henry against the Pope and to pass laws making Henry the Supreme Head of the Church. The Pope excommunicated Henry VIII.

C   *(left)* Sir Thomas More was a friend and advisor of Henry VIII. He was executed in 1535 for refusing to accept the king as Head of the Church

Henry VIII's motives

Henry wanted a divorce
His Spanish wife Catherine of Aragon had given birth to many children, but the only one to survive was a girl called Mary. Henry wanted a son. Henry believed that because Catherine had once been married to his dead brother Arthur, God had cursed his marriage. By 1527 Henry was worried because his wife was too old to have more children. Henry asked the Pope for permission to divorce his wife. The Pope refused.

Henry wanted more money
He had spent huge sums of money on fighting foreign wars and building palaces. After the Crown, the Church was the wealthiest landowner in the kingdom. This was especially true of the monasteries. If Henry controlled them he would be rich.

Henry wanted to control the Church
The Church had great power. Ever since the quarrel between Archbishop Becket and King Henry II in 1170, the Crown had struggled with the Church over who the bishops and priests should obey; the Pope or the king? Henry feared the Church might support the Pope and turn against him. Henry believed that if he controlled the Church instead of the Pope, it would make him more powerful.

Henry wanted a son and heir
He believed that a country could be strong only if it was ruled by a king. Henry wanted to marry Anne Boleyn. She was young and had promised him a son. In 1533 she became pregnant. Henry was convinced the child would be a son. He asked the Pope to allow him to marry Anne. The Pope said no.

---

1 Look at the following possible causes for Henry VIII's break from the Roman Catholic Church. List them in order of importance by putting the most important first. Then explain how the causes were linked.
   i) The Pope would not give Henry a divorce.
   ii) Henry was jealous of the power and wealth of the Church.
   iii) Henry's wife Catherine was too old to have more children.
   iv) The Pope refused to allow Henry to marry Anne Boleyn.
   v) Henry wanted a son and heir.
   vi) Henry thought his daughter Mary would not make a good queen.
   vii) Anne Boleyn was pregnant.
   viii) Henry was short of money.
   ix) Cromwell's advice to the king.

2 Read and look at sources A, B and C.
   a) Which of the sources suggest Henry expected some people to object to him making himself Head of the Church?
   b) Which of the two men executed was a Protestant? Give a reason for your choice.
   c) Why do you think Henry had no choice but to execute his friend?

3 Use a dictionary and the Glossary on page 80 to help you. Find and explain the meaning of the following words:

Protestant   reform
excommunicate   heresy
persecution

> *Found the prior at that time [11 a.m.]
> in bed with a woman ... both were
> naked.*

C A monastery in London

> ... there was no pot, nor pan, nor monk
> in the said house except one who
> boards [lives] in the town ... I intend to
> suppress [close] the ... house ...

D Monmouth Priory in Wales

> *[The abbot] delighted much in playing
> at dice and cards, and ... spent much
> money [on it], and in building for his
> pleasure. He did not preach openly.*

E Bury St Edmund's Abbey in
Suffolk

> We write in support of the said house
> of Woolsthorpe. The abbot is well
> beloved, ... having eight religious
> persons, being priests of ... good
> conversation and living.

F Woolsthorpe Abbey in
Lincolnshire

> *... the voice of the country is that while
> you have monks ... you shall have
> neither good rule nor good order there; I
> hear such sayings by the common people
> of all the houses of monks that you have
> [in] Wales.*

G The report of John Vaughan one
of Cromwell's inspectors in south
Wales

The monasteries are closed down

The new Supreme Head of the Church in Wales and England, King Henry VIII, set about making changes. Historians call these changes the **Reformation** or the Reform of the Church. The most important of Henry's changes in the Church was the dissolution (closure) of the monasteries and nunneries.

This was an enormous task. There were 9,000 monks and nuns living in more than 800 **religious houses** in Wales and England. The monasteries and nunneries in Wales were often small and poor but in England there were many which were larger and wealthier. Between them they owned over a quarter of all the land in the kingdom. Their annual income was greater than the king's. The monasteries and nunneries often helped the poor and sick and provided rest for travellers.

Thomas Cromwell convinced Henry that as Head of the Church he should have control of this wealth. Henry liked this idea. He was always short of money.

The king did not trust the monks and nuns. Henry believed that most of them still thought of the Pope as their leader rather than him. Cromwell told the king that the monks might oppose him.

A Thomas Cromwell (c.1530s)

B Monks and nuns made three vows

Chastity:
*I promise to
have nothing
to do with the
opposite sex*

Poverty:
*I promise to give
up all my possessions
and to stay poor*

Obedience:
*I promise to obey
the Pope and the
Abbot*

This worried Henry so he decided to close down the monasteries.

The king and Cromwell realised that they needed a reason to close the monasteries. So in 1535 Cromwell sent out handpicked teams of inspectors to report on the state of the monasteries and nunneries. Cromwell wanted his inspectors to provide him with evidence to show how greedy, uncaring and corrupt the monks and nuns had become.

Cromwell's inspectors reported that some monks were lazy and pleasure seeking. Others were disobeying the rules of the monastery. The inspectors found monks with wives and children and even some pregnant nuns! Some of the worst cases reported came from Wales. Robert Salusbury, the abbot or chief monk of Valle Crucis, was found guilty of highway robbery. In Strata Florida, a monk called Dan Richard was punished for forging money. Despite this, not all reports were bad, but Cromwell was only interested in reading those that were.

After reading the reports Henry decided to use Parliament to help him close down the monasteries. He was afraid that to close every religious house at once might be unpopular. So in 1536 an Act of Parliament closed down all the smaller religious houses. By 1540 the larger houses were also shut.

Five abbots opposed the king; all were hanged in their monasteries. In the north of England thousands of people rebelled. This was called the Pilgrimage of Grace. It was led by a lawyer, Robert Aske. He hoped to persuade the king to get rid of Cromwell and to reopen the monasteries. The rebellion was savagely crushed and the leaders hanged.

By 1540 all religious houses had been closed down. All their wealth and property went to Henry VIII. Some of the monks and nuns got pensions, many others did not.

H A photograph of Tintern Abbey in Wales (1993)

I A modern artist's impression of what Tintern might have looked like before dissolution

1 **Write about the part played by each of these people in the closure of the monasteries:**
  a) **Henry VIII;**
  b) **Thomas Cromwell;**
  c) **John Vaughan;**
  d) **Robert Aske.**

2 **Read source B. Which one of these vows would most worry the king? Explain why.**

3 **Read sources C to G. Which source[s] suggest[s] that:**
  a) **Some inspectors were listening to rumour and local gossip in order to write their reports;**
  b) **Some monasteries were suffering from a shortage of monks;**
  c) **Some monks were breaking their vows of poverty and chastity;**

  d) **The closure of the monasteries might not have been as unpopular in Wales as it had been in England? Explain your answers.**

4 a) **Which of the reports listed in sources C to G would Cromwell not have been interested in? Why?**
  b) **Does the evidence in these sources prove that the monasteries were corrupt and should be closed down?**

5 **You are an inspector. Using the information in the text and sources write a report for Cromwell. In your report:**
  a) **Find and use evidence to describe how monks and nuns were not living as they should;**
  b) **Suggest to Cromwell what action he should take to deal with them.**

5 $\mathcal{P}$oor Edward and Bloody Mary

B Some Catholic wall paintings and stained glass windows have survived. The church at Breage in Cornwall (c.1460-90)

The whole number burned during the reign of Mary amounted to 284. There were burnt 5 bishops, 21 ministers, 8 gentlemen, 184 farmers, servants and labourers, 46 wives and widows, 9 girls, 2 boys and 2 infants.

C John Foxe printed these figures in his *Book of Martyrs* (1563)

A certain Rogers was burned publicly yesterday. Some of the onlookers wept, others prayed to God to give him strength to bear the pain, ... others threatened the Bishops. I think it would be wise not to be too firm against Protestants, otherwise I forsee that the people might cause a rebellion.

D A letter by the Spanish Ambassador in London, Simon Renard, to King Philip (1555)

In 1547 Henry VIII died. The throne passed to his nine-year-old son Edward. Poor Edward was a sickly child. He was too young to rule the country so a council of nobles was set up to govern for him. Its leader was Edward's uncle, the Duke of Somerset.

Somerset believed that Henry VIII's changes in the Church had not gone far enough; he wanted a Protestant Church. Edward had been brought up a Protestant and, as king, was Head of the Church. With his support Somerset began making changes in the services and beliefs of the Church.

The Catholic Church did not allow priests to have wives and children. Under Edward priests were now allowed to marry. Catholic churches were decorated with colouful paintings and stained glass windows. Protestants liked their churches to be plain and simple so Somerset ordered the altars, statues and pictures to be removed. Catholic prayer books were in Latin, so a new Prayer Book in English was introduced. All services in the Church were changed from Latin to English.

For the first time the people of England could understand the church services. The people of Wales could not. In Welsh churches English replaced Latin; the Welsh language was ignored. To Welsh people, English was just as foreign as Latin. They could not understand either language, but at least they were used to Latin. This upset the Welsh.

Some members of the council were unhappy with Somerset, so he was replaced by the Duke of Northumberland. Northumberland wanted to make sure that Wales and England would become Protestant countries. However, in 1553 at the age of 15 Edward VI died.

A Painting of Edward VI and the Pope (c.1548)

The throne passed to his 37-year-old half-sister Mary. The daughter of Henry VIII's first wife Catherine of Aragon, she was a **devout** Roman Catholic. Northumberland was executed and the Protestant reforms of the Church brought to an end.

Queen Mary had disagreed with her father's reform of the Church, but she hated her brother's Protestant changes. She was determined to restore the Roman Catholic Church. Mary made the Pope the Head of the Church again. The New Prayer Book was banned. Church services changed once more, this time from English to Latin. Priests were forced to part with their wives, and those who refused were thrown out of the Church. Mary believed that people who became Protestants were committing a sin. To save their souls she believed that they had to be encouraged to return to the Catholic faith; by force if necessary. Many of those who refused were executed by being burned at the stake.

Three people were burned in Wales. Robert Ferrar, Bishop of St Davids was burnt at Carmarthen; Rawlins White, a fisherman, was burnt at Cardiff; and William Nichol, a labourer, was burnt in Haverfordwest.

By the time of her death in 1558, Bloody Mary had become unpopular. She had hoped that the public burning of **heretics** would persuade people to turn against the Protestant faith; it did not. Her marriage to the Catholic ruler of Spain, Philip II, upset her subjects. They distrusted foreigners, especially Spaniards. There was a rebellion led by a Protestant, Sir Thomas Wyatt, but it failed.

... he sent ... to his wife and willed her ... send unto him his wedding garment, meaning a shirt, which afterwards he was burned in ... Thus dies this godly and old man, Rawlins [White] for ... God's truth.

E John Foxe: *Book of Martyrs* (1563). A martyr is someone who dies for what they believe in

F The execution of Thomas Cranmer, the Protestant Archbishop of Canterbury

We have been turned by the faith of the English, our hearts will never return to their rightful place ... Your temples [monasteries] have, hither and thither, all gone in to the hands of laymen; and your churches everywhere are nothing but empty corners ... Destroying the altars once so privileged ... ; having despoiled God and his house.

G A poem by the Welsh bard Thomas ab Ieuan ap Rhys (undated)

---

1 Read the first paragraph and look at source A. Answer the following questions in sentences:
a) Who is the man in the bed?
b) Which figure is King Edward?
c) Who is being crushed by a copy of the English Bible at the bottom of the picture?
d) Was this picture painted by a Protestant or a Catholic? Explain your answer.

2 List all the changes in religion you can find in this chapter.

3 Read the text and source C.
a) How many Protestants were burned in
   i) Wales;
   ii) England?

b) Compare the figures. What do they tell us about the spread and popularity of the Protestant faith in Mary's kingdom?

4 Look at and read sources C to G.
a) List the sources which were written or drawn by
   i) Protestants   ii) Catholics
   How did you decide?

b) What evidence is there in the sources to show how cruelly the Protestants were treated by the Catholics during Mary's reign?

c) Which of the sources show that the Protestant faith may have been unpopular in Wales? Explain your answer.

6

Elizabeth and the Protestant Church

A   Elizabeth expressing her opinions on religion (c.1559)

B   Elizabeth's choices

1. To follow the example of her father and restore an English and Welsh Catholic Church with her, rather than the Pope, as its head.
2. To follow her brother and have a completely Protestant Church.
3. To continue the Roman Catholic Church of her sister.
4. To set up a new Church that would please both Catholics and Protestants by combining parts of both traditions.

In 1558 the last of Henry VIII's children, Elizabeth, became ruler of Wales and England. She was faced with many problems. The most serious of them was religion.

Elizabeth was a Protestant but she knew that many of her subjects were not. The nation was split between Catholics and Protestants. In France the hatred between Catholic and Protestant had led to bloody civil war. Elizabeth wanted to avoid this happening in her kingdom.

Elizabeth realised her people were divided and tired of all the changes in the way they worshipped. What was she to do? She had four choices (source B).

Elizabeth chose the fourth option, to set up a new Church. She knew it would not be easy to persuade the Catholics to accept her. With the help of her chief minister, Sir William Cecil, and with the support of Parliament, Elizabeth set up the new Church.

Parliament passed the Act of Supremacy making her the 'Supreme Governor of the Church'. Elizabeth had chosen a clever title. Catholics could believe, if they wished, that the Pope was still the leader of the Church. A new Prayer Book was introduced. It was based on the Protestant prayer book used during her brother Edward's reign. All prayers and services would be in English. And priests were once again allowed to marry.

The Church set up by Elizabeth was more Protestant than Catholic. It satisfied the majority of the people but not all. Some Catholics were not prepared to accept the new Church. They wanted Elizabeth's Catholic cousin, Mary, Queen of Scots, to rule

C   **Painting ordered by Elizabeth (c.1560). It is full of symbolic meanings**

them. In 1569 there was a rebellion in the north of England. It is known as the Rebellion of the Northern Earls. Elizabeth defeated the rebels.

This did not stop the Catholics from plotting against Elizabeth. They were encouraged by the Pope who excommunicated Elizabeth in 1570. He ordered her subjects not to obey her but to support Mary instead. To help them the Pope sent hundreds of specially trained priests to persuade the people to remain or become Catholics. Of these, 64 were Welshmen. The queen felt threatened.

Elizabeth thought she could rely on the Protestants. She was wrong. Although most supported her, some believed the queen was a traitor. These were known as **Puritans.** They got this name because they wanted to **purify** the new Church. They did not approve of Elizabeth's changes; they were not Protestant enough. They did not agree with the bishops running the Church. They wanted more preaching and different prayers.

Puritans hated Catholics. They were angry with the queen because they thought she was being too tolerant towards the Catholics. They wanted to persecute them. Elizabeth would not. Elizabeth decided to act. Parliament passed a new law in 1581 which said that anyone not going to church would be fined £20. If anyone failed to pay the fine they would go to prison. Those who continued to oppose the queen risked being charged with **treason.** If found guilty they were executed.

A number of Catholic priests were executed along with some Puritans. The first Catholic to be executed in Wales was Richard Gwyn, a school teacher from Llanidloes. He was executed at Wrexham in 1584 for spreading Catholic ideas. One of the most famous Puritans to be executed was also a Welshman, John Penry. He had been to Oxford and Cambridge Universities where he became interested in religion. He criticised Elizabeth and her government for ignoring the shortage of preachers in Wales. In 1593 he was found guilty of spreading Puritan ideas and was executed in London, aged 30.

D Elizabeth's chief minister, Sir William Cecil, Lord Burghley (c.1580s)

Reign	Monarch	Executed
1485-1509	Henry VII	24
1509-1547	Henry VIII	81
1547-1553	Edward VI	2
1553-1558	Mary I	284
1558-1603	Elizabeth I	5

E The number of people executed for heresy in Wales and England between 1485 and 1603

---

1 Read source A.
   a) Rewrite Elizabeth's statements in your own words.
   b) Why do you think Elizabeth's Protestant and Catholic subjects would have been happy to hear these words?

2 Read the text and answer the following questions and exercises in sentences:
   a) Who were the Puritans?
   b) Why were they a problem for Elizabeth?
   c) List the reasons why Elizabeth did not trust the Catholics.
   d) Find and write down two similarities between Catholics and Puritans.

3 Read source E.
   a) How many people were executed for heresy by the Tudors?
   b) Who suffered the most: Protestants or Catholics?
   c) In what way does this source support what Elizabeth said in source A? Explain your answer.

4 In your opinion, who was the greater threat to Elizabeth: the Puritans or the Catholics? Give reasons for your answer.

An 18p Post Office stamp (1988)

WIlliam Morgan. Cyfieithydd y Beibl
Cymraeg cyntaf 1588.
Translator of the first complete Bible into
the Welsh language 1588.

That the Bishops of Hereford, St David's, Asaph, Bangor and Llandaff shall take order ... that the whole Bible, ... as is now used in this realm in English, to be truly and exactly translated into the Welsh tongue.

B   **The Act for the Translation of the Bible (1563)**

For although it is much to be desired that the inhabitants of the same island should be of the same speech and tongue ... there can be no doubt that similarity ... in religion rather than in speech much more promotes [encourages] unity.

C   **First page of William Morgan's Bible (1588)**

... [and now not three years past], we have had the light of the gospel, yea the whole Bible, in our native tongue, which in [a] short time must work great good in the hearts of the people ...

D   George Owen, a Pembrokeshire gentleman and author: *Dialogue of the Government of Wales* (undated)

The Bibles are translated

In 1536 an Englishman named William Tyndale was executed by King Henry VIII. His crime had been to translate the Bible into English. In 1588 a Welshman named William Morgan was rewarded by Queen Elizabeth I. His achievement had been to translate the Bible into Welsh. Morgan is a Welsh hero, but fewer people are interested in Tyndale. There is a huge difference in the way these men were treated by their Tudor monarch. Why?

Henry the Catholic feared change, Elizabeth the Protestant did not. William Tyndale lived at a time when it was dangerous to be too different. He supported Martin Luther's Protestant ideas. Protestants believed that it was important to have the Bible translated from Latin into a language the people could understand. By understanding what was being read to them in church the people could feel closer to God. The aim of Protestants like Luther and Tyndale was to educate people so they could read the Bible for themselves.

The Catholic Church was against this. It argued that it was the priest's job to explain the Bible to the people. In a ceremony called the Mass the priest led the people in prayer and taught them about God. Since the priest was the only one who could understand Latin, without him there would be no religious service. This made the priest and his Church powerful. They controlled the people but after 1534 the king, Henry VIII, controlled the Church. This made the king very powerful. Tyndale's ideas threatened this power. He was **exiled** and later put to death.

E   **The burning of William Tyndale in Flanders (1536). His last words were 'Lord open the king of England's eyes'**

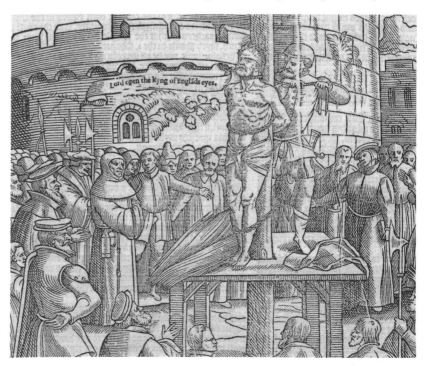

During Edward's reign there was a change. In 1547 he ordered that every church in the kingdom should have a copy of the Bible in English. It was to be read aloud every Sunday. The English Bible became so popular that when Edward's Catholic sister Mary became queen in 1553, she dared not get rid of it.

In Wales the English Bible was not popular. The majority of the Welsh people spoke only Welsh. They understood neither Latin nor English. Few of them had ever heard of Luther or Tyndale. Even fewer understood why the Tudor monarchs were making changes in the Church.

This worried Elizabeth. She realised the Welsh might not accept her new Church. This could prove dangerous. In Tudor times anyone who did not have the same religion as the monarch was seen as a possible threat.

In 1563 Parliament passed an Act for the Translation of the **Scriptures** into Welsh. Elizabeth gave two Welsh scholars, Richard Davies, Bishop of St. David's, and William Salesbury, the task of producing a Welsh Bible within five years. This was a massive task. They set to work and in 1567 the New Testament in Welsh appeared. However, Davies and Salesbury quarrelled and the work came to an end. A whole Bible in Welsh had to wait.

During the 1570s a young cleric and scholar, William Morgan, began work on translating the Old Testament. Morgan was a busy vicar in a poor parish so much of the work was done in his spare time. The work was slow and hard taking nearly 20 years to finish.

In 1588 the Bible was ready. With the help of the Archbishop of Canterbury, John Whitgift, the Bible was printed in London. Elizabeth ordered that the Welsh Bible be placed in every church in Wales. All church services and prayers in Wales were to be in Welsh. It was hoped the Welsh would become loyal Protestant subjects of the queen. Elizabeth's plans succeeded.

F Title page of William Tyndale's New Testament (1534). This copy belonged to Anne Boleyn

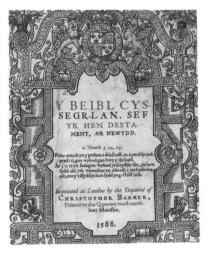

G The title page of the first Welsh Bible (1588)

1 a) Draw a timeline for the years 1530 to 1590. Use 2 cm for each decade.
  b) Mark on your timeline each date and the event mentioned in the text.
  c) Which date and event do you think was the most important in the story of the translation of the Welsh Bible? Explain your choice.

2 Read the sources. Which of the sources:
  a) Shows that William Morgan is still remembered today?
  b) Suggests that the translation of the Bible was welcomed in Wales? Explain your answer in each case.

3 a) What did Tyndale mean by his last words spoken at his execution in source E?

  b) What two clues in source G show that the Bible was printed with the queen's approval?
  c) Look at a map of Wales and England and then read source B.
  i) In what present-day Welsh counties will you find Bangor, St Asaph, St David's and Llandaff?
  ii) Find Hereford. What do you find so unusual about the queen's order to the Bishop of Hereford? How would you explain it?
  d) In your own words, explain what William Morgan was saying in source C.
  e) When do you think source D was written by George Owen? Say why?

7

Rich and poor in Tudor and Stuart society

 People knew who and where they were in life

After the monarch and royal family, the most powerful people in the kingdom were the nobles. They were rich landowners with titles like baron, earl, marquess and duke. Those nobles who often attended the monarch's court were known as **courtiers.** They joined the royal family in feasts, dances, hunting and other major events.

Below the nobles were the gentry. The most important of them had titles like knight and baronet. The most powerful even attended the royal court. Like the nobles, they owned their land and lived in large houses. They did not work for a living but employed others to work for them. Their income came from farming the land they owned.

Both groups served the monarchy in peace and war. They commanded the army and navy and helped run the government. The most powerful nobles and gentry were chosen to advise the monarch. They became councillors and sat in the Privy (private) Council.

Attending court and serving the monarch in important jobs was expensive. Many nobles and gentry remained at home to run their estates. Others helped to govern their counties. They became Justices of the Peace and sheriffs. They helped to keep law and order.

> *No people in the world is so curious [of new fashions] as [the English]. So it is very difficult to know who is noble, who is a gentleman and who is not. For those who are [not] noble or gentry go daily in silks, velvets, satins and such like. This causes great confusion.*

B Philip Stubbes, esquire: *The Anatomie of Abuses* (1583)

> *First he must be affable [pleasant] and courteous in speech and behaviour. Secondly, he must have an adventurous heart to fight but that for very just quarrels. Thirdly, he must be endowed [possessed] with mercy to forgive the trespasses of his friends and servants. Fourthly, he must stretch his purse to give liberally unto soldiers and unto them that have need; for a niggard is not worthy to be called a gentleman. These be the properties of a gentleman, which whosoever lacketh deserveth ...the title of a clown or of a country bore.*

C (right) Sir William Vaughan of Llangyndeyrn's description of a seventeenth-century gentleman. Published in his book *The Golden Grove* (1608)

Sir Richard Bulkeley of Beaumaris, knight ... was a goodly person fair of complexion and tall of stature ... He was temperate [moderate] in his diet, not using tobacco or drinking of healths ... He never changed his fashion but always wore round breeches and thick bumbast doublets though very gallant and rich. Being demanded why he followed not the fashion his answer was that people were given so much variety and change that once every seven years they would return to his fashion ... He was no great scholar, but a great reader of history ... [He was] understanding in matters belonging to housekeeping, husbandry, maritime affairs, and building of ships and maintaining them at sea. He was so singular in his conceit that he always drew his own letters and answered all letters with his own hand ... He was a great housekeeper and entertainer of noblemen ... His estate in Anglesey was worth £2,500 per annum, in Caernarfonshire £800 and in Cheshire £100, having always a great stock of ready money lying in his chest ... He kept many servants [and] he never went from home without 20 or 24 to attend him. He was a great favourite of Queen Elizabeth. He had powerful friends at Court, and had the gentry and commonality of the country at his service.

 William Williams, gentleman, historian from Anglesey: *History of the Bulkeley Family* (1674)

Since the time of Henry VII and Henry VIII ... the gentlemen ... in Wales have [been] brought up ... at the universities of Oxford and Cambridge ... where some prove to be learned men. The people are grown to be of great wealth, the gentlemen of great livings, so that ... some ... doth receive yearly £500, some £300, and many £100.

E George Owen, esquire: *The Dialogue of the Government of Wales* (1594)

F A portrait of Sir Walter Raleigh with his son, dressed in the latest fashion (1602)

---

1 **Read the text and sources. Find and list as many:**
   a) similarities   b) differences
   between the nobility and the gentry.
   c) Using the information in source A to help you, list the writers of sources B, C, D and E, in order of their gentry status (importance).

2 **Read source B, C, D and E. How does source D:**
   a) agree   b) disagree
   with the other sources?
   Make a list in each case.

3 **Read source D.**
   a) How reliable is source D as information on the Elizabethan gentry? Explain your answer.
   b) The queen is considering appointing Sir Richard Bulkeley to join her Privy Council. She has asked you to advise her on this matter. Draw up a profile (outline) of the man to include information on name, status, address, physical description, education, habits, interests, skills, occupation, total annual income, etc. You can include additional information if you wish.

A portrait of Sir John Perrot
(Undated but thought to be 1583)

Sir. JOHN PERROTT
Knight of the Bath
Lord Lieut.* of Ireland.
1583.

An affluent [rich] man, when days were fair
I made some money, here and there,
And then I came to London town
To look it up, to look it down.
Of boon companions there was no dearth [shortage]
They welcomed me with joyous mirth,
They lured me to the dens of vice,
And taught me how to play at dice.
Stripped of my wealth I then began
The journey home, a saddened man.

B Thomas Prys was another young Welsh gentleman who found London too much of a temptation. He wrote a poem describing his experiences (c. 1590s)

Sir John Perrot, a Tudor gentleman (1528-92): a case study

There were few nobles in Tudor Wales. Apart from William Herbert, Earl of Pembroke, the earls of Essex, Leicester and Worcester were Englishmen who spent little time in Wales. They often employed others to run their Welsh estates for them.

By far the largest group of landowners in the country below the nobility were the gentry. The vast majority of them were Welsh and they lived on their estates. One of the richest and most powerful was Sir John Perrot.

Perrot's family had lived in Pembrokeshire for nearly 250 years. He was born in 1528 at the family home of Haroldston near Haverfordwest. Perrot was educated at the Cathedral grammar school at St David's. It was a Protestant school so his religious education would have been in the new faith. His best subjects at school were languages; he was able to speak French, Spanish and Italian. He could also read and write Latin.

In 1546 when he was 18 Perrot left home for London. There he began a three-year **apprenticeship** in the household of the Marquis of Winchester, the Lord Treasurer of England. This was a great honour for Perrot. Here he would learn the rules of being a gentleman.

However, because of his hot temper, he also learned how to fight. On one occasion Perrot and his fellow apprentice, Henry Neville, Lord Abergavenny, quarrelled. Before they could be separated they broke 'glasses ... about one another's ears [so that] blood besprinkled ... the chamber'. Perrot became a popular member of London

C Carew Castle, Sir John Perrot's favourite home. He also owned Laugharne Castle and at least ten other manor houses in south Wales

society. Soon he was introduced to the young King Edward by whom he was knighted a few days after his twenty-first birthday.

Unfortunately for Perrot it seems he was easily dazzled by the bright lights of London. He tried to keep up with his wealthier friends, but he was soon in debt. In a letter to his mother he wrote of his reckless spending on 'the tilt (jousting) and other toys I am ashamed to tell'. Besides jousting his favourite sport was hunting.

Perrot also enjoyed life as a soldier. During Mary's reign he fought against the French and in Elizabeth's reign he fought the rebellious Irish. Here he proved that although he was brave he could also be reckless. In an attempt to crush the rebellion of the Irish lord James Fitzmaurice, Perrot swore to 'hunt the fox out of his hole'. Once being drawn into a trap he found himself outnumbered twelve to one, but he still refused to surrender! Luckily his cavalry arrived in time to save him.

Perrot also spent some time as a ship's captain. He had the task of defending the seas around Wales and Ireland from the Spanish. As Vice-Admiral of south Wales he was expected to crush the pirates that operated there. He was once accused of being a pirate himself.

Perrot took his role as a gentleman seriously. He knew that he had certain responsibilities like helping to govern the county. He became **sheriff** of Pembrokeshire in 1551 and chief Justice of the Peace in 1562. He became mayor of the town of Haverfordwest three times and represented the people of Pembrokeshire in Parliament.

In 1583 the Queen appointed him Lord Deputy of Ireland. At the Tudor court, Ireland was known as the 'graveyard of reputations' because it had destroyed so many ambitious men. It was a difficult and dangerous country to rule. But Perrot knew the Irish, he had been Lord-President of Munster for three years during the 1570s. For four years Perrot worked hard to govern the Catholic Irish fairly. He succeeded.

The Queen rewarded him by appointing him to the Privy Council. However, others were jealous of his success. He was accused of treason, found guilty and sentenced to death. He died a prisoner in the Tower of London before the sentence could be carried out.

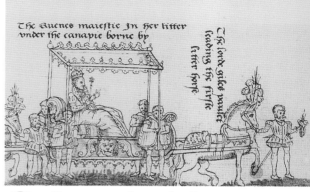

D Perrot was chosen by Queen Elizabeth to be one of the four gentlemen who carried the canopy of state at her Coronation in 1559

E Portrait of Dorothy Perrot (c.1590s). At the age of 18 she ran away with Sir John's son Thomas and married him in 1583. She was the daughter of Walter Devereaux, Earl of Essex

1 a) **Through how many monarchs' reigns did Sir John Perrot live? List the monarchs with the dates of their reigns.**
   b) **Find and list one important event in Perrot's life which occurred in each monarch's reign.**

2 **Study the portrait of Sir John Perrot (source A).**
   a) **What information can you obtain from the picture about Sir John Perrot?**
   b) **What doesn't the portrait reveal about him?**

3 **You have written a biography (life story) of Sir John Perrot. Design a dust cover for the book and include the following:**
   the title;
   an illustration;
   a brief summary of its contents.

A   William Harrison: *A Description of England* (1577)

B   *(below)* **Portrait of a London Merchant (1532)**

Towns and merchants

Tudor and **Stuart** towns were fewer in number and smaller than today. They were usually tightly packed with buildings, the streets were long and narrow and there were few large open spaces. The largest space within the town was usually reserved for the twice weekly markets and fairs. By the Tudor period craftsmen had established permanent shops to sell their wares and to supply the daily needs of the **urban** inhabitants.

Many towns were attached to castles so that they were surrounded and defended by high walls. This was particularly true in Wales where most of the towns had been built by the English. Their aim had been to keep the Welsh out. During the Middle Ages the Welsh were allowed to enter the town by day to trade but they were not allowed to live there. They had to leave by nightfall or risk arrest. By the sixteenth century this had changed. Towns which had once been English like Caernarfon, Harlech and Conwy became almost completely Welsh.

Towns were important because they were centres of trade and **commerce.** Countryfolk regularly attended the towns' weekly markets and fairs to buy and sell. Some were important as centres for learning and for new ideas. Larger towns like Carmarthen, Brecon, Bangor, Ruthin and Abergavenny had established grammar schools during Elizabeth's reign.

The majority of the people who lived in the towns were known as **burgesses.** This meant they were members of the town's trading community, which gave them certain rights and privileges. During the Middle Ages they had formed **guilds** to protect their particular

C   *(below)* **A modern artist's reconstruction of what the town and castle of Cydweli might have looked like in the fifteenth century. By 1550 the town's population had risen from 300 to 1,200**

trade or craft. These guilds still existed in Tudor times but they were less important. After 1563, local JPs, instead of the guilds, fixed wages and set the rules of service for apprenticeships. By 1700, guilds were in decline and only 50 towns in Britain had them.

Apprenticeships were still the best way for ambitious young men to learn a trade. During Elizabeth's reign an apprenticeship was set to last seven years. It was tough being a young apprentice. The hours were long, the pay poor and very often they had nowhere but the shop to sleep. Despite this apprenticeships were highly prized. Between 1532 and 1542 there were 1,202 apprentices in Bristol: 400 were local, 528 came from other parts of England, 100 came from Ireland and 174 were Welsh.

Towns were often unhealthy and dangerous. Plagues and diseases like the sweating sickness tended to break out regularly. Crime and drunkeness were also problems.

Thomas Botesworth is fined 2p because he is a common brawler and disturber of his neighbours and to give him warning to leave it or else he is to be carried in a dung cart about the town ... and then to be put in the stocks.

Agnes Osier alias Beggar of Brook Street, spinster, for breaking into the house of William Reynolds [merchant] in the night time, and stealing two flaxen sheets worth 22p and £3 in money ... to be hanged.

E Extracts from JP's court files in Essex (1588-99)

D Picture of a busy market place (Flanders in the late sixteenth century)

F *(right)* A fifteenth-century merchant's house in Tenby

1 Answer the following questions in full sentences:
   a) What made towns so important?
   b) What information in the text suggests that apprenticeships were popular?
   c) Why were many towns in Wales attached to castles and surrounded by high walls?
   d) What effect might these walls have on the growing prosperity of towns like Cydweli (source C)?

2 a) Read source A. To which class did William Harrison belong?
   b) Suggest why the different classes of people he describes took their lunch and dinner at different times of the day.
   c) How does the first paragraph on page 28 and source C help to explain why towns were so unhealthy?
   d) Explain why the crimes described in source E were more likely to occur in towns rather than in the country.
   e) Look at source B. Explain why an historian might think the man was wealthy.

3 a) Explain the meanings of these words:

   urban   commerce   apprenticeship
   guild   burgess

   b) Write a description of life and work in a typical town during the early seventeenth century. Use source D to help you and use each of the above words in your essay.

A beggar is punished (1577)

Margaret ferch Ieuan ap David ap Madog of Ffestiniog in the county of Merioneth, spinster, at Clynnog ... stole a cheese worth 1p and money to the value of 2p being the property of Lewis ap John ap William.
... it is adjuged by the Justices that she shall be flogged and thereafter she is to be nailed by her ear in the market place at Caernarfon.

B Court record from the Caernarfonshire Quarter Sessions (1557)

There are many thousands in these parts who have sold all they have even to their bed-straw, and cannot get work to earn money. Dog's flesh is a dainty dish, and found upon search in many houses.

C A gentleman from Lincolnshire reported on the famine caused by the failure of the harvest (1623)

The Problem of the Poor

The Tudors faced a growing problem; poverty. Nearly half the population of Wales and England lived in real poverty during the sixteenth and seventeenth centuries. Some were so desperately poor that they either begged or stole food to live on, or died of starvation. Why?

There have always been poor people. During medieval times the poor had been helped by the Church and the charity of the monasteries. Many of them had been able to get some casual work on the land especially at harvest time. Outbreaks of disease and plague, such as the Black Death, had the effect of reducing the number of poor people. Medieval monarchs were fond of war and they often employed thousands of men, rich and poor alike, to fight in their armies. There was a problem but medieval society seemed to cope.

All this changed in the sixteenth century. Henry VIII closed all the monasteries down and reduced the wealth of the Church. It could no longer provide the poor with enough charity.

Rich landowners wished to make greater profits from their land. They changed from **arable** to **pastoral** farming because it was cheaper and required less workers. To help this they enclosed the large open fields with fences and hedges. Many former tenants and labourers were forced out of their homes and their jobs.

War was an expensive business. Although Henry VIII continued to fight wars his children, Edward, Mary and Elizabeth, were happy to avoid them. Armies were reduced and ships scrapped.

There was a rise in prices and in the population. More people with no work and less charity caused serious problems. Even those who were lucky to find employment found it hard to live. Prices were rising faster than wages. This is inflation; it also meant disaster.

D A modern drawing showing the punishment suffered by Lewis Griffyth. He was an 18-year-old convicted of vagrancy in Monmouth town (1577)

What did Tudor governments do about the problem of the poor?

Between 1531 and 1601 Parliament passed a series of Acts which it hoped would solve the problem. Here are some examples of what the Acts said.

E 1531:
This law said that any fit man or woman who was found to be a wandering beggar, rogue or vagabond and could not explain him or herself was to be tied up, stripped near naked and whipped through the town. In 1536 beggars were licensed.

F 1547:
This law tried to make it easier to spot already convicted vagrants or vagabonds by branding them with a V-shaped hot iron. If they were caught again they were forced to become slaves for two years.

G 1562:
By this law the government encouraged people to contribute to the cost of dealing with the poor.

H 1572:
Vagrants were to be whipped and bored through the ear with a hot iron or nailed to a tree for a first offence. They were to be executed for a third offence. Everyone in the parish was forced to contribute money to the Poor Rate.

I 1601:
This Poor Law tried to make the task of solving the problem easier and cheaper. It included all the previous laws but added that there were three types of poor people;

1   The fit or able-bodied poor who were put to work in the parish;

2   The old, sick or crippled poor who were looked after in almshouses;

3   The idle or criminal poor who were to be sent to houses of correction after punishment. Serious criminals were to be executed.

J   (below) A Tudor gentleman and a licensed beggar (undated)

Alas it has been a hard summer of three months; corn is expensive and poverty has been [forced] upon us.
It is not remarkable how, in such dire circumstances,
the oppressive rich are able to benefit by it all.

K   A poem by the Welsh bard Edward ap Raff on the famine of 1597

---

1 Please read the text and sources.
   a) Find as many reasons as you can to explain why the number of poor people increased during the Tudor and Stuart period. Take a full page and present your reasons in the form of a spider diagram. Remember to use pictures and words.
   b) Which of the reasons listed best explains why poverty increased? Explain your choice.

2 a) Explain the meanings of the following words and phrases:

   inflation   vagrancy   famine
   licence   almshouses   Quarter Sessions

3 a) You are a beggar brought before a JP having been caught begging a second time. Write a speech in your defence.
   b) You are a JP. Justify the sentence you will pass on the beggar.

4 What can we learn from sources A to K about:
   a) The attitude of the Tudor government to the poor?
   b) The methods used by the government to deal with the poor?

8 Threats to the kingdom

Parliament wanted her to marry. They
felt the country would be safer if she did
... She knew that, if she married an
English nobleman, she would offend
others. If she married a foreigner, she
would not have been so free to follow
her own policies.

A J F Aylett: *The Making of the
United Kingdom* (1992) - a school
textbook.

B Mary with her infant son James.
After Mary fled Scotland the
Protestant lords made him king

In 1562 Elizabeth fell ill with smallpox and nearly died. This
posed a serious threat to the safety of the kingdom. She was not
married so she had no children. If the queen had died who would
rule? (See page 80 for the family tree of the Tudors).

Elizabeth's closest relative and heir was Mary, Queen of Scotland.
But she was a Roman Catholic and a friend of France, England's
enemy. The thought of Mary as their queen frightened Elizabeth's
ministers. When Elizabeth recovered from her illness they tried to
persuade her to marry. She refused.

Mary was nearly ten years younger than her cousin so she was
prepared to wait. Elizabeth thought that as long as she stayed
healthy and Mary remained in Scotland the problem of her
succession could be forgotten. However, some of Elizabeth's
Catholic subjects would not forget. They believed that Mary was
their rightful queen. But they kept quiet and did nothing; until 1568
that is!

Mary's rule in Scotland had been a disaster. The Scots were
mainly Protestant and they did not trust their Catholic queen. They
were upset when she secretly married an English Catholic, Lord
Darnley. Although she gave birth to a son and heir called James, the
marriage was doomed.

Darnley was a foolish, hot-tempered man who had murdered
Mary's friend David Rizzio. In 1567 after just two years of marriage,
Mary's husband Lord Darnley was killed. Many people believed that
Mary and her close friend Earl Bothwell were guilty of his murder.
When they married three months later, the Protestant lords
rebelled. Mary's army was defeated and she fled to England for
safety.

Mary's presence in England posed a serious threat to Elizabeth
and her kingdom. But what was she to do? Elizabeth had three
options:

1 She could send Mary back to Scotland. If she did this Mary's
Scottish enemies might imprison her or worse, execute
her. Elizabeth would feel responsible for the death of a fellow
queen and her heir.
2 Mary could be sent to France. This worried Elizabeth because
France was a powerful enemy. Mary might gather an

The Queen of Scots is and shall always be a dangerous person
to you. Yet there are degrees of danger. If she is kept a prisoner
... It will be less, if at liberty, greater.

C Sir William Cecil, Elizabeth's chief minister, wrote to her
in October 1569

army large enough to invade England as well as Scotland.

3 Elizabeth could imprison Mary in England. If this happened English Catholics might plot or rebel against their Protestant queen.

Elizabeth chose the third option - to imprison Mary in England. Was she right? A month later some powerful earls from the north of England rebelled. The rebellion was crushed. A few months later in 1570 the Pope **excommunicated** Elizabeth.

Between 1571 and 1587 there were four plots to **assassinate** Elizabeth: the Ridolfi Plot (1571), the Throckmorton Plot (1584), the Parry Plot (1585) and the Babington Plot (1586). Fortunately for Elizabeth, the chief of her secret service, Sir Francis Walsingham, discovered them and the plotters were executed. Mary was proving to be far too dangerous a threat to Elizabeth's life. Something had to be done

Since that guilty woman [Elizabeth] ... is the cause of so much injury to the catholic faith ... there is no doubt that whoever sends her out of the world ... does not sin but gains merit ... And if ... English gentlemen decide actually to under take so glorious a work, [you] can assure them that they do not commit any sin.

D Pope Gregory XIII wrote to his ambassador in Spain (1580)

(below) The views of Elizabeth I and Mary, Queen of Scots

ELIZABETH R — MARY R

Elizabeth: "I am Queen and will remain Queen...even if you have to die..." 1558 / ?

Mary: "I should be Queen and will be Queen ...when you die..." ? / ?

---

1 a) Write a diary entry for Elizabeth the day after Mary arrives in England. You are trying to decide what to do with her.

b) Work in groups. You are Elizabeth's councillors. Discuss the options listed on these two pages; which one would you advise her to take? (You may think of another option). Give reasons for your choice.

2 Answer these questions in sentences:

a) Why was Elizabeth's illness in 1562 thought to be such a threat to the kingdom?

b) Find two ways in which Mary's reign as Queen of Scotland had been a disaster.

3 Read sources A and D. What can you learn from them about:

a) Why Elizabeth refused to marry;

b) Why the Pope became Elizabeth's enemy;

c) Why English Catholics were prepared to plot against or even kill the queen?

A A contemporary drawing of the execution (Antwerp, 1587)

One of the women put a holy cloth over the Queen of Scots' face, and pinned it fast to her hair covering. Then the Queen knelt down on the cushion and spoke aloud a psalm in Latin. She laid down her head. Lying quietly upon the block and stretching out her arms, she cried aloud in Latin, 'Into your arms, O Lord', three of four times... One of the executioners held her slightly with one of his hands and she received two strokes of the axe, making small noise or none at all. He lifted up the head for all to see and said 'God save the Queen!'

B Report to William Cecil, Lord Burghley, February 1587

The Execution of Mary Queen of Scots

Parliament asked Elizabeth to execute the 'monstrous huge dragon', as they called Mary, Queen of Scots. Elizabeth refused. She was unwilling to have a relative and a fellow monarch killed; unless it could be proved that Mary was involved with the plots to kill her. Walsingham set out to provide the evidence.

Walsingham's agents trapped Mary by pretending to be friends who wanted to free her and make her queen. After 19 years of imprisonment Mary was desperate enough to listen to them. A Catholic gentleman, Sir Anthony Babington, and Mary's former secretary, a Welshman, Thomas Morgan, were drawn into the plot. They wrote to Mary of their plan to kill Elizabeth. Mary agreed to the plan in her letters. Unknown to them their letters were being **intercepted** and read by Walsingham.

Babington was arrested and executed in September 1586. Soon after, Mary was put on trial and found guilty. Elizabeth reluctantly signed the death warrant some months later. In February 1587 Mary was executed.

Jane Kennedy bound the Queen's eyes with a white cloth ... Mary knelt down on the cushion in front of the block ... placing her chin ... the Queen stretched out her arms and legs and spoke in Latin, 'In Manus tuas Domini' three or four times. Mr Bull's assistant steadied the body ... The first blow missed the neck and cut into the back of the head ... her lips moved ... the second blow gashed her shoulder blades. Eventually the neck was severed by using the axe as a saw. It was about ten a.m. The executioner held aloft the severed head crying 'God save the Queen'... The lips continued to move for a quarter of an hour after her death ... the auburn tresses [hair] in his hand came apart from the skull and the head fell to the ground.

C Antonia Fraser: *Mary, Queen of Scots* (1969)

1 a) **Why did Elizabeth not wish to execute Mary?**
   b) **Explain why it might have been better to have killed Mary secretly and pretend she had died a natural death, perhaps from illness?**
   c) **Who do you think was most responsible for causing Mary's execution: Sir Francis Walsingham, William Cecil (Lord Burghley), Elizabeth I, Sir Anthony Babington or Mary herself? Give reasons for your choice.**
   d) **Do you think Mary deserved to be put to death? Explain your answer.**

2 a) **Read and compare sources B and C. From your comparison, list any similarities and differences between the two sources.**
   b) **How would you explain the differences?**
   c) **Look at source A. When you compare source A with sources B and C there are differences in the way they describe Mary's execution. Find and write down at least three differences.**

3 **If you were asked to write an account of the execution of Mary, Queen of Scots, which one of the above sources would you choose? Give reasons for your choice.**

The Spanish Armada

In July 1588 a fleet of 140 warships set sail from Spain. The fleet's commander, the Duke of Medina Sidonia, had been given the task of invading and conquering England and Wales. The man responsible for planning the invasion was Philip II, king of Spain.

Why was Philip so determined to attack Elizabeth's kingdom? Philip had a personal grudge against Elizabeth. He had once been Mary Tudor's husband and after her death, in 1558, he had asked Elizabeth to marry him. Philip was upset when she refused.

For ten years English privateers had been attacking Spanish ships, looting their treasure and raiding towns in Spain's American Empire. Elizabeth publicly criticised her sea captains but secretly encouraged them. The final insult came in 1587 when Sir Francis Drake sunk 30 Spanish ships in Cadiz harbour and boasted that he had 'singed the King of Spain's beard'. Philip was furious.

The two monarchs disagreed over religion. Philip was a Roman Catholic but Elizabeth was a Protestant. He wanted England and Wales to become Catholic again; by force if necessary. She helped the Protestant rebels in the Spanish Netherlands fight for freedom against Philip.

Philip said that he wanted to avenge the execution of Mary, Queen of Scots. She was a fellow Catholic whom he believed had been murdered by a Protestant queen. Because he received the blessing and support of the Pope, Philip was convinced that God was on his side. As his 'Invincible Armada' set out to punish the **heretic** Elizabeth, Philip had no doubt that he would win.

Just before the Armada sailed Philip published details of his invasion fleet. They were printed and sold all over Europe, including England.

 A contemporary portrait of King Philip II (1556)

The sailing of the Armada should be delayed ... to allow the weather to grow milder ... To me it seems that a sovereign with such a reputation in the world would not allow himself to be swept away by a thirst for vengeance ... Should your majesty ... accept my advice I would still recommend that the rumour ... be circulated that the fleet is to sail at once, with a view to frightening the Queen.

 A Spanish nobleman, Marquis de Santa Cruz writes to Philip of Spain (1587)

 Ships: 140 (110 warships and 30 supply ships)
Men: 30,480 (8,500 sailors, 19,000 soldiers, 2,800 galley slaves and 180 priests)
Arms: 2,600 cannons, 123,000 cannon balls, powder, armour, swords and pikes
Victuals: Biscuit, bacon, fish, cheese, rice, beans, wine, vinegar and water

1 a) List as many reasons as you can find to explain why Philip wanted to invade England and Wales. Write each reason separately.
  b) From your list, which reason do you think King Philip would have chosen to justify his invasion? Explain your answer.

2 Read sources B and C.
  a) What does source B suggest may have been the reason for the invasion?
  b) What do you believe to have been the real reason for the invasion?

3 Read source C.
  a) This kind of information would be kept secret today. Why do you think Philip was so keen to publish it?
  b) Which part of source B would you use to support your previous answer? Write it down.
  c) Protestant printers in England published this information, but they added such things as thumbscrews, whips, racks and pincers. Why do you think they did this?

The route of the Spanish Armada

Why did the Armada Fail?

Philip's plan seemed so simple. The Armada was to sail to the Netherlands, collect the Duke of Parma's army, land the army in Kent and then march on London. Philip believed that 25,000 English Catholics would rise up and support his invading army. With their help Queen Elizabeth would be captured and replaced with a Catholic ruler. England and Wales would become part of Philip's Spanish Empire. Without English help the Protestant rebels in the Netherlands would quickly surrender.

When the Armada sailed through the English Channel, the English commander Lord Admiral Howard, sent 50 ships to attack the Spaniards. They failed to get close enough to do any serious damage to the enemy. Despite four separate running battles in the Channel, the Armada reached Calais safely. Only one ship had been lost to English gunfire.

> *The English, with their excellent ships, fought not at all according to the custom ... keeping at a great distance did fire upon the hull and sails of the enemy.*

D Petruccio Ubaldini was an Italian Protestant living in London: *The Story of a Glorious Victory* (1590)

The truth is that the Armada was short of men and equipment. It did not have enough soldiers to attack England directly; nor did it have enough ships to pick up the Duke of Parma's troops. It was short of powder; the wine was going off; the fish went rotten.

B J F Aylett: *The Making of the United Kingdom* (1992) - a school textbook

> *Even if the Armada supplies us with the 6,000 Spaniards as agreed ... I shall still have too few troops ... It will be necessary for us to fight battle after battle. I shall, of course, lose men by wounds and sickness ... In a very short time my force will be ... reduced as to be quite [unable] to cope with the great multitude of enemies.*

E Duke of Parma writes to King Philip (1588)

C *(right)* The Spanish fleet sailing in the shape of a crescent. This is what made the Armada invincible. The strongest warships sailed on the rim protecting the slower supply ships in the centre. If the fleet was attacked from the rear then the horns closed in and destroyed the enemy ships

F This painting shows the English and Spanish fleets fighting in the English Channel. It was painted in 1588/89

Medina Sidonia expected the Duke of Parma to be waiting in Calais with the soldiers. Parma was not there. The Armada had to wait until the two Spanish commanders could arrange to meet.

In the meantime, the English were busy planning their next move. On land, the Earl of Leicester gathered an army at Tilbury near London ready to fight the Spaniards if they set foot in England. Queen Elizabeth joined him and spoke to the troops (Source G).

At sea Lord Howard and his two chief captains, Drake and Hawkins, came up with a clever plan (see source H).

The *hell-burners* (fireships) worked. The crescent formation was broken. The panic stricken Spaniards sailed out of port to face the waiting English fleet. Medina Sidonia had no choice but to sail his ships where the wind was blowing them: north.

I … am resolved in the midst and heat of battle to live and die amongst you … I know I have the body of a weak and feeble woman, but I have the heart and stomach of a king, and a king of England too, and think foul scorn that Parma or Spain … should dare to invade the borders of my realm.

G Elizabeth's speech (1588)

[The Lord Admiral] found eight small ships and set them amongst the Spanish fleet on fire. The enemy not only had to break his sleep but the fire coming so suddenly upon him, he cut his cables to let slip his anchor.

H Petruccio Ubaldini (1590)

The Spanish fleet was conquered … not by the men nor by the ships … It was defeated by the weather … Only against the hurricane and the gales did we lose.

I Ortiz Munoz, a Spanish historian: *The Glorious Spanish Empire* (1940)

J *(left)* This medal was made to celebrate the victory. The Latin words mean 'God blew and they were scattered'

---

1 Read sources D and H.
How reliable is Petruccio Ubaldini's evidence? Give reasons for your answer.

2 Read source D and look at source F.
a) How do sources D and F contradict (disagree with) each other?
b) Read source G. Why did Elizabeth I go to Tilbury?
c) What does her speech tell you about her character?

3 What does source J tell us about how Elizabeth and her government saw the events? Why was it important to claim that God was involved in the victory?

4 In your opinion which was the greater threat to Elizabeth and her kingdom:
a) Mary, Queen of Scots?
b) The Spanish Armada?
Give reasons for your choice.

5 Write an essay explaining why the Armada failed.

9 *T*he Spanish fleet of Wales

In order to qualify for an annual licence to trade they were required to be literate, numerate, married householders aged above 30. But they also needed to be rugged, hard-fisted, and intrepid [daring] men. Little romance belonged to droving. It was a filthy and dangerous occupation. [They] provided farmers with much-needed currency [money] and acting as local bankers …

A Geraint Jenkins: *The Foundations of Modern Wales* (1987)

B A modern painting showing cattle being driven along the many drovers' roads that were first opened during the Tudor period. In many cases these were the only roads to be found in Wales

Spain was one of the richest countries in Europe. Her wealth came from the gold and silver shipped from her American Empire to the king of Spain's treasury. Wales was one of the smallest and poorest countries in Europe. Her wealth came not from precious metals but from the sale of **livestock.**

Much of the land in Wales was given over to pastoral farming. Welsh farmers realised that the uplands were better suited to keeping cattle and sheep rather than for growing crops. During the Tudor period sheep were more important than cattle. The sheep were kept to supply wool for the English cloth industry. However, by the end of Elizabeth's reign the demand for Welsh wool had fallen. The cloth industry was in decline.

During the Stuart period many Welsh farmers turned to keeping more cattle than sheep. Because of the increasing population there was a greater demand for Welsh meat. This was particularly true of the growing English towns and cities. By 1688 London's population had risen to 475,000. The problem was how to get the cattle to English markets. The answer was the drover.

Most drovers were well-to-do men who travelled Wales buying cattle and other livestock from Welsh farmers. The cattle were taken to villages like Llangefni in north Wales and Llandovery in the south, where they would be shod for the long journey. Thousands of cattle were driven to England each year and sold to English dealers at the great cattle fairs. The most famous cattle fair was at Smithfield near London. The dealers then fattened the cattle on the rich English pasture before killing them for meat.

The cattle industry and the drovers became very important for the economy of Wales. Many farmers and small village communities

depended on the drovers to sell their livestock. They would trust the drovers to take their cattle, sell them in England and then return to Wales with the money. Only then would the Welsh farmers be paid. Sometimes the sums collected were so great that drovers were tempted to run away with the money.

However, most of the drovers were honest men. Some of them were men of great learning. Edward Morris of Perthi Llwydion in north Wales was a well-known poet while Dafydd Jones of Caeo in the south was a famous hymn-writer. A few were rich men. When he died in 1736, Thomas Lewis of Trefeibion Meyrick in Anglesey left £1,500 in his will.

Most Welsh people could only dream of travelling to London. They knew little of what was happening in the outside world. They often asked the drovers to buy goods for them from London shops, which they could not get locally. They brought mail, news and details of new fashions.

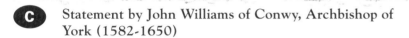

The Spanish fleet of Wales which brings hither the little gold and silver we have.

C Statement by John Williams of Conwy, Archbishop of York (1582-1650)

E *(left)* A photograph of an inn called the Drover's House at Stockbridge, Hampshire, England. The drovers usually slept at inns and alehouses along the route. Many of them came to be named after the Drovers who used them. This alehouse was unusual in that it had the following Welsh words inscribed on the wall: *Gwair Tymherus-Porfa Flasus-Cwrw Da-a Gwal Gysurus* (Temperate Hay-Tasty Grazing-Good Beer-and a Comfortable Bed)

1 Write out and complete these sentences, choosing the right answer from each set of brackets:
   a) The Welsh economy relied upon the trade in (gold and silver/livestock) for its wealth.
   b) Most of the land in Wales was used for (arable/pastoral) farming.
   c) During the sixteenth century Welsh farmers kept more (sheep/pigs) than cattle.
   d) The biggest demand for Welsh wool came from the (European/English) cloth industry.

2 From the text on page 38, write down one example of change and one of continuity (something that stays the same) in farming.

3 Read and look at sources A to E. List at least four benefits which the drovers brought to Wales.

4 You are a wealthy cattle trader who wishes to employ a drover to take your livestock to England. Use the information in the text and source A to help you.
   a) Design an advertising poster to attract the right applicant;
   b) Write a job description for a suitable candidate.

IO Explorers and privateers

A   David Fraser: *The Adventurers* (1976)

When Henry VII won [the] throne at Bosworth in 1485, Wales stood on the fringe of a world that was changing. In seven years' time Columbus would land in the West Indies and Wales would thereafter be at the centre of the western world.

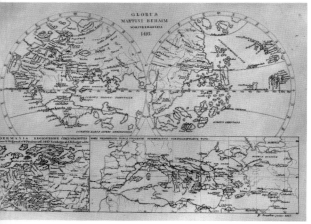

B   (*above*) **A map of the world dating from the fifteenth century**

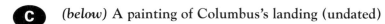

Christopher Columbus was not a Welshman and he did not sail from Wales. It is likely that he had never even heard of this little country, but the Welsh were soon to hear of him. His discovery of a New World beyond the ocean changed the Old World forever.

Before Columbus's journey of exploration people thought their world looked like the map shown in source B.

Columbus did not try to prove this map wrong, he agreed with it. He did not intend or expect to discover a new land, he 'bumped into' America by accident. His aim was to discover a new route to the East. He believed that it was possible to sail west across the Atlantic Ocean to reach China in the east. Spices and other luxury goods came from there. The man who discovered this route would become rich and famous.

Many people disagreed with Columbus, some thought he was mad, others were afraid. They said he would fall off the edge of the world or be eaten by great sea monsters. Columbus said he did not believe these stories.

Such an expedition would be very expensive. The kings of Portugal and France refused to give him money. Henry VII, king of England, was very interested but before he could give his answer Queen Isabella of Spain agreed to lend Columbus the money. In return he promised her new lands and gold. To get the support of the church Columbus promised to spread the Christian faith.

With a crew of 90 men, some of whom were criminals, and 3 small ships called the *Nina*, *Pinta* and *Santa Maria*, Columbus set sail on 3 August 1492. After nearly ten weeks of sailing his men

C   (*below*) **A painting of Columbus's landing (undated)**

were ready to **mutiny.** They were afraid. They had not sighted land. Columbus tried to calm them and agreed to sail on for two or three more days. He was lucky.

On the morning of the 12 October a sailor on the *Pinta* spotted land. Columbus went ashore to explore the island he named San Salvador which means Holy Saviour.

The natives did not look like the Chinese he was expecting to see. After three months' sailing around other islands in the area he thought that he must be near India. European travellers had heard of India but did not really know where it was.

Columbus returned to Spain from the islands he called the 'West Indies'. He brought back little gold, but he did bring some Indians and parrots to prove that he had discovered a new route to the East. Queen Isabella and her husband King Ferdinand were pleased. They paid for more expeditions. Columbus never found the gold or spices he was looking for. He never even realised that he had found a new continent. But others soon did.

In 1507 a new map of the world was made by a German called Waldseemuller which showed this new continent. But instead of naming it after Columbus it was named after another sailor called Amerigo Vespucci. Other countries wanted to share in this new knowledge of the world. In 1497 Henry VII employed another Italian, John Cabot, to sail further north than Columbus. He discovered a new island off the coast of what we now call Canada. He named it Newfoundland. But perhaps the most famous of these new explorers were Ferdinand Magellan and Vasco da Gama of Portugal. In 1498 da Gama found a route to India by sailing south along the coast of Africa. Magellan discovered the Pacific Ocean and, although he was killed during the expedition, some of his men completed the first voyage around the world between 1519 and 1523.

DE PISCIB. MONSTRO.

De suffocatione nauium per monstrosos Pisces.

D Contemporary drawing showing the sea monsters feared by sailors

1 **This is a question about motives (why people did things).**
   a) **The following is a list of motives to suggest why Columbus made his voyage:**
      i) **fame**
      ii) **wealth**
      iii) **to spread the Christian religion**
      iv) **the need to explore**
      Explain which one you think persuaded Columbus?
   b) **Which of the above motives does source C suggest persuaded Columbus?**
   c) **What motives did King Ferdinand and Queen Isabella have in supporting Columbus? Explain your answers fully.**

2 a) **Put this list of explorers onto a time-line.**

   Vasco da Gama 1498
   Christopher Columbus 1492
   Ferdinand Magellan 1519
   John Cabot 1497

   b) **Write a sentence on each of the explorers to say why they should be remembered.**

3 **Some historians have called these voyages of discovery an Oceanic Revolution. Would you agree with this historical label? Give reasons for your answer.**

A An account written by a Spaniard, Gaspar de Vargas, of Drake's landing near the town of Guatulco on Mexico's Pacific coast (1579)

On 15 April [1579] he put into port at Guatulco, his last contact with the Spaniards on that remarkable voyage ... he sailed northwards [and] found a fit and convenient harbour on the Californian coast ... Drake took possession of this land in the name of the Queen and called it 'Nova Albion'... [he] made a number of [visits] inland to discover the nature of the terrain [land] and the natural life that might be found there.

B An account of Drake's voyage written by an English historian, Alex Cumming (1987)

Two Englishmen explore the world: Drake and Cook

Life at sea was tough and dangerous. Ships, supplies and a trained crew were expensive. The kings of Spain were wealthier than the monarchs of England so they continued to send expeditions to the New World. After the death of Henry VII, the Tudors sent very few. While Spanish sailors became famous as explorers, English sailors found fame as **privateers.**

This meant that sea captains like Francis Drake, John Hawkins and Martin Frobisher were licensed by Queen Elizabeth to steal from Spanish treasure ships. They became famous for their courage and daring. They even raided towns along the coast of Spain's Empire in the Americas. The Spaniards called them pirates, but they claimed to be explorers.

In 1577 Drake set off with five ships and a 164-man crew on a voyage of exploration. He had four main tasks:

1 to become the first Englishman to sail around the world
2 to discover new lands and claim them for the queen
3 to bring back gold, spices and other riches
4 to show the Spanish that they did not control the oceans

In 1580 Drake returned to a hero's welcome. He brought back great wealth worth nearly £250,000 for which the queen gave him a knighthood and £10,000. She took the rest.

By the time of Captain James Cook's birth in 1728 Britain ruled the seas. Her navy protected the expanding British Empire which had grown rich on trade. France had replaced Spain as Britain's main rival but her fleet was no match for the Royal Navy. Conditions on board ship had changed little since the days of Drake. The ships were larger and there was more room for the crews, but still many died from disease. The most dangerous was scurvy. This was caused by a lack of vitamins. Cook was one of the first captains to fix the diet of his sailors to include fresh fruit. Scurvy soon disappeared.

Sea captains like Cook were very different from those like Drake. Cook was not interested in plunder but in science and **navigation.** He became friends with members of the Royal Society some of whom, scientists and astronomers, joined him on his voyage in 1768. As captain of the *Endeavour* Cook explored the Pacific Ocean and mapped the coasts of Australia and New Zealand. These he claimed for King George III.

C *(left)* Portrait of Sir Francis Drake, painted in miniature after his return from his voyage (c.1581)

There were still lands to be discovered and trade routes to find. The most prized was the Northwest Passage. This was a sea route believed to connect the Atlantic Ocean with the Pacific Ocean north of Canada. Like Frobisher and Hudson before him, Cook failed to find it but he was one of the first to explore the Antarctic.

Columbus, Drake, Cook and others like them are remembered because they dared to explore where most people were afraid to venture. They opened up the world and increased our knowledge of it.

D *(right)* Drake's ship the *Golden Hinde*

E The Search for New Trade Routes and Lands

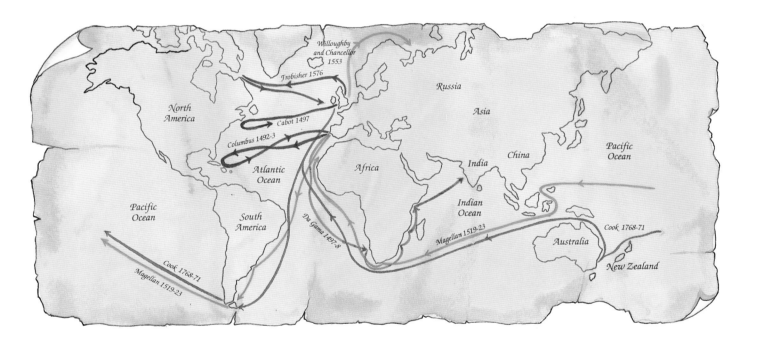

1 a) **List four reasons to explain why Francis Drake set out on his voyage in 1577.**
  b) **Which, in your opinion, was the most important reason for Drake's voyage? Use evidence from the text and sources to help you explain your choice.**
  c) **Give two reasons to explain why Captain Cook set out on his voyage in 1768.**
  d) **Compare the careers and achievements of Drake and Cook. Find and list three ways in which they were similar and three ways in which they were different.**

2 **Read sources A and B.**
  a) **How do the sources contradict (disagree with) each other?**
  b) **How would you explain this contradiction?**
  c) **Which source do you think is the most reliable account of Drake's expedition to the New World? Explain your answer.**

3 **If you were writing a book about great English heroes, who would you choose to include; Captain Drake or Captain Cook? Explain your choice.**

Madoc ... finding ... that his native country was ... to be turmoiled in a civil war, did think it better ... to try his fortune abroad; and ... leaving North Wales in a very unsettled condition, sailed with a small fleet of ships ... to the westward.

He came at length to an unknown country, where most things appeared to him new and uncustomary, and the manner of the natives far different from what he had seen in Europe. [Therefore] this country was discovered by the Britains [Welsh] long before either Columbus or Americus Vesputius sailed thither.

 In 1584 a priest and historian called Dr David Powel published his book *Historie of Cambria, now called Wales*

 Portrait of Thomas Prys [1604]

Welsh adventurers abroad

If we are to believe the story told in source A, then America had not been discovered by an Italian sailing in a Spanish ship in 1492 but by a Welshman sailing from Porthmadog in 1170. Unfortunately, the adventures of Prince Madog are nothing more than legend. But it shows how impressed the Welsh were by Columbus's voyages and how keen they were to explore the world.

During the sixteenth century most Welsh adventurers did not have ships of their own so they sailed with English sea captains. They were privateers rather than explorers. In 1567 Richard Williams, Humphrey Roberts and Thomas Ellis sailed with Captain John Hawkins to the New World. They had been licensed by the queen to plunder Spanish ships and towns.

By the 1580s some Welshmen had been promoted to captain their own ships. The best known and most colourful of them was the gentleman sailor-poet Thomas Prys from Plas Iolyn in north Wales. He behaved more like a pirate than a privateer. Often he would keep the cargo he stole from Spanish ships rather than hand it over to Queen Elizabeth.

In 1583 Prys and his close friends Piers Griffith from Llandegai and William Middleton from Llansannan seized and kept a rich cargo of tobacco. They were the first to smoke tobacco in public. When not at sea Prys spent his time in London, drinking, gambling and brawling. He wrote a poem describing his life in London. By 1595 Prys had had enough excitement and returned home for good. He died in his bed at the age of 70 in 1634.

Two of the most feared pirates in the seventeenth and eighteenth centuries were Sir Henry Morgan from Gwent and Bartholomew Roberts from Pembrokeshire. Morgan was 19 years old when he ran away from home. Morgan's rise to fame and fortune was rapid.

He was brave and daring but cruel. He destroyed Spanish towns and stole much wealth. In a short time he had become successful, wealthy and well-known. In 1674 Charles II knighted him and made him deputy-governor of the British island of Jamaica. It was thought better to have him as a friend than as an enemy.

Yet it is to Bartholomew Roberts, nicknamed Black Bart or *Barti Ddu*, that we owe the well-known pirate flag. He was the first to use the 'skull and crossbones' in 1718. Black Bart struck terror into the hearts of the English and Spanish settlers in America and the West Indies. But like most pirate captains Black Bart met his end in battle, fighting a British warship in 1722. It was his wish to be buried at sea dressed in all his fine pirate clothes.

Henry Morgan of Abergavenny, labourer, bound to Timothy Tounsend of Bristol [merchant] for three years to serve in Barbados

C Entry in the *Bristol Apprentice Books* (1655)

He served his time in Barbados [seven years], and, obtaining his liberty [freedom] he took himself to Jamaica, there to seek new fortunes ... there he came by two ships belonging to pirates. They were both ready to sail and because he had no work he went with them. After 3 or 4 expeditions he had learnt the trade ... by his valour [he] raised himself to what he now is.

D An author called John Esquemelling wrote about Morgan: *History of the Buccaneers (Pirates)* (1684)

Because I squandered [wasted] all I had,
Because she made me slightly mad,
I do most earnestly desire
That [London] be consumed by fire.

E An extract from Thomas Prys's poem, 'An ode to show that London is Hell!' *(Cywydd i ddangos mai Uffern yw Llundain)*

F A sketch of Sir Henry Morgan (1635-88)

I sailed across the stormy main
And half the world to far-off Spain,
Thinking that there would be for me
Vast stores of treasure out at sea.
I bought a ship, I sold my land
To get the means for what I planned.
I gathered men with much ado
To sail - they were a wicked crew.
Some dark skinned Jews as well,
Strong-stomached men, from Hell.

G An extract from one of Thomas Prys's poems describing his life as a pirate (undated)

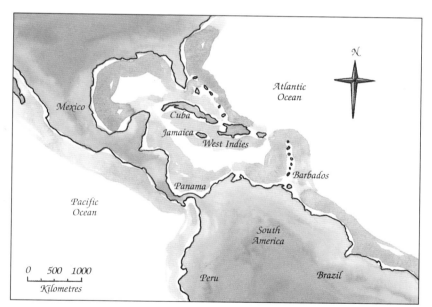

H A map of the Caribbean

---

1 Read sources A, D and G.
   a) Why do you think Dr David Powel made up the story of Prince Madog discovering America?
   b) Explain why Thomas Prys and Henry Morgan became pirates.
   c) How useful are these sources for someone studying the role of the Welsh as explorers and pirates?

2 a) Explain why Henry Morgan was honoured and rewarded by King Charles II.
   b) Why did Thomas Prys retire from piracy?
   c) In your opinion do Prys, Morgan and Roberts deserve to be remembered as criminals or heroes? Give reasons for your answer.

Who rules? Monarch and Parliament in conflict

A Portrait of James I of England and VI of Scotland (1621)

Britain is a **democracy** which means that the people have the freedom to vote for the government of their choice. The elected government meets in Parliament in London. It takes the decisions and makes the laws that govern Britain. So today Parliament has the power to rule the country.

In the sixteenth century the country was governed by the monarch and a small group of ministers. These ministers were not elected but chosen by the monarch. They met as the monarch's Privy Council.

Parliament was less important. It met only when the monarch needed advice or money. The monarch could ignore Parliament's advice but could not ignore its power to raise taxes. The question of money sometimes caused Tudor monarchs to quarrel with their Parliaments.

Parliament's importance began to change during Henry VIII's reign. In 1529 the king turned to Parliament for help in his quarrel with the Pope over his divorce. Parliament agreed to pass a series of Acts or laws which ended the power of the Pope and allowed Henry to become Head of the Church in Wales and England. With Parliament's support the Tudor monarchs had become more powerful than previous kings or queens of England.

Parliament now had the power to pass laws as well as raise taxes. Even so, the monarch still made the decisions. Parliament could not meet without the monarch's permission.

Elizabeth used Parliament less than her father had done. When it did meet she kept control by using her feminine charm and by skilful management. Her successor King James I was not so charming or skilful. James had been used to Scottish Parliaments. They caused no trouble and did as they were told. He soon found the English Parliament was different.

The Members of Parliament (MPs) came to believe that they should have a greater say in the government of the country. They had clashed occasionally with Elizabeth over this belief, but the queen was usually able to win them over. Elizabeth had been popular, James was not. The king had upset them by refusing to discuss matters which he believed were none of their business. Worse, he upset Parliament by declaring his belief in **Divine Right.** Since he was chosen by God to rule he could do as he wished. Anyone who disagreed with him was considered a **traitor.**

Parliament and its MPs had fought hard during Elizabeth's reign to establish the right to speak freely in Parliament without fear of arrest. They now demanded the right to discuss any matter which they believed affected the government or the people of the country. The king refused. The scene was set for conflict.

B The House of Lords at the opening of Parliament (1523). The king sits on the throne in the centre; his two Archbishops sit to his right. Below them are the bishops in red and the abbots in black. On the king's left sit the nobles. The Commons and their Speaker, Sir Thomas More, stand in the top right of the picture

C *(right)* Sir Thomas Smith's descriptions of the Houses of Parliament: *De Republica Anglorum* (1565)

The first day of the Parliament and the Prince and all the lords in their robes of Parliament do meet in this higher house … Next under the Prince sitteth the Chancellor, who is the voyce … of the Prince. On one side of the house … sitteth the archbishops and bishops … on the other side the dukes and barons.

… the knights of the shire and the burgesses of the Parliament, … are called by such as it pleaseth the Prince to appoint … to which they answer and declaring for what shire or towne they answer; then they are [asked] to choose an able man to be the mouth of them all …

The most high and absolute power of the realm of England consisteth in the Parliament. For every Englishman is intended to be there present, … [who]soever he be, from the Prince (be he king or queen) to the lowest person in England. And the consent of the Parliament is taken to be every man's consent.

No reviling [abuse] or nipping words must be used. For then all the House will cry, 'It is against the order'; and if any speak [rudely] against the Prince or the Privy Council, I have seen them not only interrupted but it hath been [decided] after to send them to the Tower.

1 **Answer the following questions.**
   a) **What were the three main functions (powers) of Parliament? Which, in your view, was the most important function? Explain why.**
   b) **Explain when and why Parliament became more powerful.**
   c) **How and why did King James I quarrel with Parliament?**
   d) **Which was the most powerful by the end of James I's reign in 1625: Parliament or the King? Explain your answer fully.**

2 a) **How might source B suggest that the House of Lords was more important than the House of Commons in the sixteenth century?**
   b) **Which House is the more powerful today: the Lords or Commons?**

3 **Read source C.**
   a) **Find three ways in which the monarch controlled Parliament. Write them down.**
   b) **How does the source suggest that Parliament was important?**

A kingdom divided

The kingdom was divided in religion. In 1605 a group of Catholic conspirators planned to blow up King James I and Parliament. They failed. All were arrested and put to death. This event is known as the Gunpowder Plot. In 1625 Charles became king and married a French princess, Henrietta Maria. This angered the Puritans because she was a Catholic.

One of Charles's closest advisors was William Laud, the Archbishop of Canterbury. Laud believed that he and his bishops ruled the Anglican Church because God had chosen them. He was determined to rid the country of Puritans. In 1637 three Puritans were punished by Laud for claiming that the Church was corrupt. Their ears were cut off, their cheeks were branded, they were fined and then sent to prison. Laud became unpopular, but the king stood by him.

The kingdom was divided in other ways also. Just like his father James, Charles believed in Divine Right. Unlike his father, Charles chose to rid himself of Parliament altogether. But Charles needed money. Parliament refused to give him what he wanted. They quarrelled and in 1629 Charles closed Parliament down.

From 1629 until 1640 Charles I ruled without Parliament. His main problem was where to get the money he needed to govern the country. He turned to the law and increased fines for many offences. These profits from justice went to the king, but it angered the people. He tried to impose new taxes and raise loans from the nobility and from abroad.

By far the most unpopular tax was Ship Money. In times past only those people living near the sea were expected to pay. This tax was designed to pay for a navy to defend the country in times of war. Although the country was at peace, Charles still expected people to pay. In 1635 he extended the tax to cover all the people living inland as well.

Some people refused to pay. In Wales a gentleman from Glamorgan, David Jenkins of Hensol, objected. In 1637 the sheriff of Cardiganshire reported that he had been unable to raise a penny in the county. In England John Hampden, a wealthy landowner, took his objection to court. He lost. People blamed the king.

In 1640 the Scots rebelled. They were unhappy with Laud's plan to enforce changes in their Church. They threatened to invade England. Charles needed money to raise an army. He had no choice but to recall Parliament. Parliament agreed to give him the money; but at a price. They forced him to execute his friend and chief minister, the Earl of Strafford. Archbishop Laud was imprisoned.

The king was presented with a list of complaints known as the Grand **Remonstrance.** This angered the king. He tried but failed to arrest the MPs who had drawn up the list. Charles ordered Parliament to close and the MPs to go home, they refused. The king decided to deal with Parliament once and for all.

E A propaganda cartoon from the 1630s

F A cartoon showing Archbishop Laud eating the ears of one of the Puritans, William Prynne (1637)

A Puritan is such another thing
As says, with all his heart, 'God save the King'.

A Protestant is such another thing
As makes, within his heart, God of the King.

A Romanist is such another thing
As would, with all his heart, murder the King.

G Extracts from a poem written in 1622

1 a) **Who do you think was responsible for publishing sources E, F and G; a Puritan, an Anglican (Protestant) or a Catholic (Romanist)? Explain your choice in each case.**

b) **Why did the authors of sources E and F publish these pictures?**

c) **How useful are these sources to an historian wishing to understand the reasons why the nation was divided in religion?**

2 **Working in groups, think about the question 'What caused the Civil War?'**

a) **Read the text. Find and list as many causes as you can.**

b) **Add your answers to question 1 to this list.**

c) **Read sources A, B and C. How do these sources help us explain why the Civil War happened?**

d) **Add your answers to question 2 b) to your list. Now rearrange your list of causes by putting the most important first. Say why you think it is the most important cause of the Civil War.**

3 **Do you think there would have been a Civil War if the Stuarts had not been kings of England? Explain your answer.**

*T*he Civil War

12

Charles I left London and made for Nottingham. Here he raised an army. His plan was to march on London, deal with the mobs who had forced him to flee the city and then arrest the MPs who opposed him.

Parliament was faced with a difficult decision; it could do as the king wanted and close down or it could fight to defend itself. Parliament chose to fight.

The idea of war upset many people. Some people did not know which side to choose, others preferred not to get involved. Parliament had 27 Welsh MPs, 20 of them supported the Grand Remonstrance. When the king refused to agree to it and left for Nottingham, their number fell to seven. When the fighting began only five Welsh MPs remained loyal to Parliament. Twenty joined the king and two went home. With the exception of Pembrokeshire and parts of Denbighshire, Wales declared for the king.

At the first battle of the Civil War, Edgehill, more than 2,000 Welshmen fought for the king. Both sides claimed victory so the war continued. The better trained and well armed Royalist cavalry won many victories in 1643. It looked as if the king might win the war. During 1644 Parliament hung on and despite winning a battle at Marston Moor it was becoming desperate. It turned to one of its best commanders for help. This newly promoted general was called Oliver Cromwell. He realised that a new army had to be created. After many months of training Cromwell's New Model Army was ready for action. In 1645 they won a major victory at the battle of Naseby. His army went on to win many more victories. They were so good that they were nicknamed Ironsides.

Unlike the Welsh, the Scots sided with Parliament. They did so not because they believed Parliament to be right but because they were paid to do so. They also believed that Parliament would protect their Protestant beliefs. On the other hand, Charles had turned to the feared Catholic Irish for help. This made him very unpopular with many people in England. The Irish army proved to be a great disappointment. With Scottish help Parliament soon defeated the Royalists. By 1646 the war was over.

In a desperate attempt to escape capture by Parliament, in May 1646 Charles surrendered to the Scots. As a Stuart king from

A King (Royalist/Cavalier) versus Parliament (Roundhead) and a map showing the areas of Wales and England they controlled in 1642

The existing law courts - the king's courts - could not try a king. Parliament would have to set up a special court.

B The view of a modern historian (1992)

I never read nor heard, that lex [law] was rex [king]; but it is common and most true, that rex is lex, for he is ... a living, a speaking, an acting law.

C Statement made by Sir Robert Berkeley a high court judge (1635)

Scotland Charles thought he could persuade them to help him. He was wrong. In return for more money, they handed him over to Parliament.

The king was imprisoned in Carisbroke Castle on the Isle of Wight while Parliament decided what to do with him. This uneasy peace lasted only a few months. In 1648 a second Civil War had broken out. Charles had made a secret deal with the Scots and they sent an army south to rescue him.

In Wales former supporters of Parliament changed sides and declared for the king. They had not received their back pay. Soon a large Welsh army was marching from Pembrokeshire towards England. Led by John Poyer, a merchant from Pembroke, Rice Powell and Rowland Laugharne, the Royalist army reached St Fagans near Cardiff. Here it fought a savage battle and lost.

The Royalists retreated to Pembrokeshire. Cromwell soon arrived with an army. Besieged by land and sea Powell surrendered Tenby. After a long siege Poyer and Laugharne surrendered Pembroke castle.

Cromwell marched north and at Preston he crushed the Scots. Soon the English Royalists surrendered also. The second Civil War was over.

Parliament blamed the king for the war. It realised that it could never trust him again. As long as he lived his supporters might cause another war. The decision was taken: the king must die.

D Contemporary sketch of Rowland Laugharne (1640s)

E (left) English propaganda pamphlets making fun of the Welsh (1640s). They were thought to be poor soldiers

1 Please read the text and sources and answer the following questions.
  a) Why might the king have felt confident of winning the war?
  b) Give four reasons why Parliament won the war.
  c) How important was Scotland's contribution to the Civil War? Explain your answer.
  d) Why did the second Civil War break out in Wales in 1648?

2 a) Which side in the Civil Wars do you think was responsible for publishing source E?
  b) How reliable is this source?

3 How do sources B and C help to explain the difficulties faced by Parliament in:
  a) charging the king with a crime
  b) putting the king on trial?

13 *T*he trial of King Charles I

This is an account of the trial of Charles I. It has been adapted from a transcript of the State Trial as reported by John Mabbut in 1649.

THIS SHOULD BE READ AS A PLAY

Westminster Hall, Saturday, 20 January 1649

JOHN BRADSHAW, an ambitious lawyer and friend of CROMWELL, is the President and Chief Judge of the High Court.
JOHN COOK is the State Prosecutor.

BRADSHAW: Silence in Court. Colonel Thomlinson, bring in the prisoner.

[KING CHARLES wearing a hat which he does not remove and carrying a silver topped cane is escorted to a red velvet chair in the centre of the hall]

BRADSHAW: Charles Stuart, the Commons of England have been empowered to try and judge you for the misfortunes that you have brought upon the nation.

COOK: Charles Stuart you are accused of ...

[The KING taps COOK's shoulder with his cane]

KING: I demand you ...

BRADSHAW: Mr Cook pray continue ...

COOK: You are accused of ruling as a tyrant, of being a traitor ...

KING: Ha!

COOK: ... and of waging war against Parliament and the people.

BRADSHAW: Sir, you have heard the charge, how do you plead?

KING: Remember, I am your king, your lawful king ... I have this position through the grace of God. Therefore, I am answerable to Him not this unlawful gathering.

BRADSHAW: You are the elected king of England and so are brought here in the name of the people of England.

KING: No Sir, I deny that. England's throne is inherited and has been for almost a thousand years. I repeat, by what authority do you try me?

BRADSHAW: Sir, you have been told already it is not your place to question the Court.

KING: This Court is illegal ... show me in the Bible or in the constitution [rules] of the Kingdom where it states you are empowered to try me.

BRADSHAW: Sir, it is obvious we are getting nowhere. The Court is adjourned.

[The king refuses to be silent].

KING: This is not a matter to be taken lightly. I have sworn to keep the peace and I have a duty to God and my country. Be sure of your authority and right in this matter or you will have to answer to God and the country.

BRADSHAW: The Court will adjourn until Monday. You will be expected to give your final answer, or the Court will proceed regardless.

KING: Why should I answer to you. You have not satisfied an ordinary man of your authority let alone your king.

BRADSHAW: That is your opinion. We the Court of judges are satisfied at our legal authority to try you.

KING: It is not my opinion or yours which should decide my fate.

BRADSHAW: The Court has noted your remarks ... take the prisoner away.

[The KING is led away and as he passes the Lord President's table he sees the mace and sword of State.]

KING: I am not afraid of that. [Looking at the sword].

VOICES IN THE PUBLIC GALLERY: God save the King! Justice! Justice!

Monday, 22 January 1649

BRADSHAW: Silence in Court. I have given instructions to the Captain of the Guard to arrest anyone who disturbs the proceedings.

COOK: May it please your Lordship that at our last sitting I accused the prisoner of high treason and other crimes. However, he did not answer the charge but disputed the authority of the Court. I propose he be directed to respond yes or no, or else his silence will be taken as an admission of guilt and the Court may proceed accordingly.

BRADSHAW: Mr Cook I agree ... if the king will not answer the charge he will be regarded as having admitted his guilt.

KING: I repeat, I do not acknowledge the power of this Court to try a king. I am not protesting on my own account but for the freedom of the people. Power without the right of law will mean that every subject in the land will be threatened.

BRADSHAW: Sir I will not allow this ... I demand an immediate and direct answer.

KING: I am no lawyer but I know as much law as the next man. I have the right to be heard.

BRADSHAW: I must remind you that you are not here to dispute our authority. Your behaviour will be recorded as contempt of Court.

KING: I will not be silenced. The House of Commons is not a Court of law and never has been. Would not I the king have been aware of it?

BRADSHAW: Call upon the king to answer the charge. [To the Clerk of the Court]

CLERK OF THE COURT: Charles Stuart, King of England, you have been accused on behalf of the people of England of high treason and other crimes.

KING: How do you plead? [Silence]

BRADSHAW: Guards take the king away.

KING: I will not leave. I will only answer the charge when I know by whose authority you try me.

BRADSHAW: ... take charge of the prisoner.

KING: ... but I require time to be heard.

BRADSHAW: It is not for the prisoner to require anything.

KING: Prisoner! I am no ordinary prisoner!

[KING CHARLES protests as he is led away]

A A contemporary drawing of the trial

---

1 a) With what crimes was King Charles charged?

b) How did he plead: guilty or not guilty?

c) How did the king show a lack of respect for the Court in the way that he behaved?

d) Do you think this behaviour was deliberate? Explain why.

e) To what was the king referring when he said 'I have this position through the grace of God'?

2 Work in pairs.

a) Discuss and list the strengths and weaknesses of primary evidence adapted and presented in this way.

b) How reliable is John Mabbut's 'true account' of the trial? Explain your answer.

Tuesday, 23 January, 1649

COOK: It is as clear as crystal that the king is guilty and I urge that judgement be made and sentence passed.

BRADSHAW: Sir, the Court would be justified in sentencing you now. Please for the last time, are you innocent or guilty of these charges?

KING: I spoke yesterday on behalf of the people of England and was interrupted. May I speak freely or not?

BRADSHAW: The Court will hear you, but you must respond to the charge.

KING: I care nothing for the charge. It is for the freedom of the people of England that I am concerned. How can I, your king, recognise a Court such as this?

BRADSHAW: Sir, you should know the decision of the Court.

CLERK OF THE COURT: [Repeats the charge] ... the Court requires you give an answer.

KING: This Court is not legal and does not represent the interests of the people. Your intentions have been written in bloody letters across the Kingdom.

BRADSHAW: Record this contempt. Soldiers, take charge of him. You have heard the findings of the Court and therefore you cannot fail to see that you are before a Court of Justice.

KING: I see I am before a power.

 Portrait of John Bradshaw (c. 1650s)

Wednesday, 24 January, 1649

Evidence was taken in private chamber.

Saturday, 27 January, 1649

VOICES IN THE PUBLIC GALLERY: Execution! Justice! Execution!

BRADSHAW: Silence in Court.

KING: I wish to be heard without interruption.

BRADSHAW: Sir, I am President of the Court. You may speak ... but later. Gentlemen [of the Court] it has been apparent that the prisoner has been brought to the Court several times in the name of the people of England to answer the charge of treason and other serious crimes.

LADY FAIRFAX: [Shouting from the gallery] Not half, not even a quarter of the people of England support this action. Cromwell is a traitor.

[LADY FAIRFAX is the wife of Sir Thomas Fairfax a general in Cromwell's army]

BRADSHAW: Guards, please escort the lady from the Court. The Court has fully considered the case and since he has not responded to the charge he must be considered guilty. Further, since the charges are so serious the Court has agreed upon the sentence. However, we are willing to hear the accused speak in his defence ... so long as he does not question the authority of this Court.

KING: If this is the case, then I will say only this. In the past few days you have taken everything away from me, but that which I value more than my life ... my conscience and my honour. If I have valued my life more than my kingdom then I should have defended myself ... I might have delayed the sentence which I know you will pass upon me.

JOHN DOWNES: Are our hearts made of stone? What sort of men are we?
[One of the Judges]

OLIVER CROMWELL: What is the matter with you? Are you insane? Sit down and be quiet.

DOWNES: I cannot be silent. If it costs me my life, I have to do it. I am not willing to agree to the sentence and wish the Court to adjourn to hear my reasons.

[Court adjourns for half an hour]

BRADSHAW:	Sir, I accuse you of breaking the contract with your people. As king you are sworn to protect your people ... but you have broken this contract, this promise. Sir, you have been called a tyrant, traitor, murderer and public enemy to the Commonwealth. I urge you to beg God's forgiveness.
KING:	Allow me to respond to such serious accusations.
BRADSHAW:	Until now you have refused to acknowledge the legality of this Court and ignored opportunities to defend yourself! Permission to speak is denied.
CLERK OF THE COURT:	[Reads the charge] ... for all treasons and crimes the Court judges that Charles Stuart, tyrant, traitor, murderer and public enemy, shall be put to death, by the severing of his head from his body.
KING:	Sir, will you allow me a word?
BRADSHAW:	It is not permitted to be heard after sentence has been passed.
KING:	No Sir!
BRADSHAW:	No Sir! Guards, remove the prisoner.
KING:	Please Sir, allow me to speak ... hold the sentence ... Sir! ... if I am not to be heard what chance of justice will my people have.

[KING CHARLES is led away]

B Painting of the execution by a French artist (c. 1650s)

C Title page of a pamphlet written by the king's executioner (1649)

1 a) **In your opinion, did Charles I have a fair trial? Explain your answer.**
b) **Which of these words best describe Charles I's character?**

arrogant   strong   thoughtless
stubborn   brave   proud

c) **How far can Charles be blamed for his own death?**
d) **Did Charles have to be executed? Were there any alternatives to killing him?**

2 a) **Do you think Charles was innocent or guilty of the crimes he was charged with?**
b) **In your opinion, did Charles deserve to be executed? Explain your answers in both cases.**

3 **Read source C. You are Richard Brandon. Based on the information given in the title page and, using your imagination, write the confession you believe he might have written shortly before his death in 1649.**

14 The king is dead, long live the ...?

A A Royalist propaganda cartoon shows Cromwell and his government working with the devil

B A cartoon showing Father Christmas (1653). The Puritans abolished the celebration of Christmas

On 30 January 1649, King Charles I was executed. Parliament and its leader Oliver Cromwell declared that monarchs could not be trusted. So Wales and England became a **republic** with no king or queen. Parliament would rule the new republic.

The Puritan MPs wasted no time in establishing their power. They abolished the monarchy, the House of Lords and the Anglican Church. But the House of Commons needed money to run the country. So they raised taxes, fined Royalists who had fought against them and sold confiscated Crown lands. This angered some people but they could do little about it. Parliament had the support of the army.

In 1653 the House of Commons and the army quarrelled. Many MPs believed that the army was becoming too powerful. The army thought the MPs had failed in their promise to improve the country.

The most powerful man in the country was Oliver Cromwell. He was an MP and a general in the army. Cromwell had become fed up with Parliament so he supported the army. Parliament was closed down and the MPs sent home.

Cromwell was offered the Crown of England. He refused. But he did accept the title Lord Protector of the Commonwealth. He did not want to rule the country as the old king had done. He believed in freedom and he wanted the people to share in the common wealth of the country. He even tried to set up a new Parliament. Cromwell also believed in religious toleration. With the exception of the Catholics whom the Puritans hated, the people were given the right to worship as they wished.

Cromwell ruled Wales and England for five years between 1653 and 1658. His government was unpopular. He upset the strict Puritans because they thought he was too tolerant. The Royalists did not trust him and Parliament refused to work with him.

Cromwell felt he had no choice but to rule with the support of the army. Some people hated this because they thought he was ruling like a **dictator.** He divided Wales and England into 11 districts, and put Major Generals in charge of each of them. Some of these military governors were strict Puritans. They tried to force

> *Cromwell had a magic quality of leadership. People - even many Royalists - trusted and admired him. Above all, people knew how successful he was; a not very important country gentleman had become ruler of a powerful nation! People thought this must be the work of God.*

C Joe Scott (1992)

the people to accept their Puritan ways and ideas. Gambling was banned so were popular sports like cockfighting, bear baiting and horse racing. Singing and dancing were forbidden and theatres closed.

On the other hand, the Major Generals kept good law and order. Cromwell made them responsible for setting up a system to educate and look after the poor. They improved prisons and set up hospitals to look after the old, the sick and mentally ill.

When Cromwell died in 1658 he was succeeded as Lord Protector by his son Richard. Richard did not want the job, nor did others want him to have it, and after a year in power he resigned. He was nicknamed 'Tumbledown Dick'. The people of Wales and England had had enough of Puritan and military rule. So Charles I's son was invited back to England to become King Charles II. The period of Republican rule, known as the **Interregnum**, had come to an end.

Some opinions of Cromwell

D A portrait of Cromwell (1649)

[Cromwell] died on 3rd September … His body being opened and embalmed his [body] was found full of corruption and filth, which was so strong and stinking … but his name and memory stinks worse.

 E James Heath, a Royalist (1663)

No man was better and worse spoken of than he … The soldiers … most highly [praised] him till he began to seek the Crown …
I think that … he meant honestly in the main, and was pious and [reasonable] in the main course of his life till prosperity and success corrupted him.

F Richard Baxter, an army officer (1696)

And something I can deliver of him upon my own knowledge, which assures me that that Man is … a coward … he is notoriously [treacherous], ambitious and hypocritical.

 G Denzil Holles, a strict Puritan (1699)

If Cromwell is not quite a national hero, he is generally recognised as a great figure in our history, the soldier - politician - who put an end to civil war, restored peace at home and respect abroad.

H C V Wedgwood (1973)

---

1 Look at sources A and B.
   a) What messages are these cartoons trying to convey to their readers?
   b) How useful are cartoons as sources of information?

2 Read sources C, E, F, G and H.
   a) Which of the sources were written by modern historians and which of the sources were written by contemporary writers?
   b) How did you decide?
   c) In what ways do the modern historians differ from the contemporary writers in their opinions of Cromwell?
   d) Suggest reasons for these differences.
   e) Which of the contemporary writers would you regard as the most and least reliable as sources of information on Cromwell?

This cartoon appeared on the front cover of a pamphlet called *The World Turned Upside Down* (late 1640s)

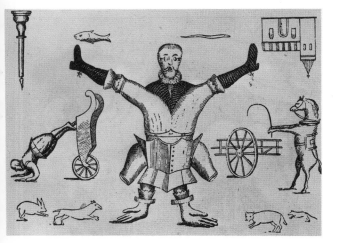

Wales under Cromwell

The Puritans were not popular in Wales. The people did not care for their religion or their strict way of life. They did not like being ruled by Cromwell, but they did nothing to stop him.

The Welsh knew that Cromwell could be very cruel to those who opposed him. Catholic Ireland had suffered terribly. The towns of Drogheda and Wexford were destroyed and more than 4,000 of their inhabitants killed. Many others were shipped as slaves to the West Indian island of Barbados.

Cromwell treated Wales differently. He thought that the Welsh were a simple people who had been led astray by the Royalist gentry. He believed that with sound teaching and good preaching they would become loyal Puritans.

In 1650 Parliament passed an Act for the Better Propagation (encouragement) and Preaching of the Gospel in Wales. This Act was important because it set up schools which enabled the people to learn about God and religion. It also taught them to read.

On the other hand, the Welsh gentry who had supported the king during the war, were treated harshly by Cromwell. Many of them were heavily fined or had their lands confiscated (taken away). Others were removed from positions of power and loyal Puritans appointed in their place.

James Berry became the Major General in charge of Wales and the English border counties. Because Berry had once been a humble clerk in a Shropshire ironworks, the rich and once powerful landowners hated him. They thought it was wrong for such low-born men to rule them. They believed that the execution of the king and the fact that men such as Cromwell and Berry were running the country had turned the world they had known upside down.

Putting the head where the rump should be
And putting the tail in the front may be,
Chopping and changing perpetually,
Making great mock of each noble degree.

B A Welsh bard wrote this poem giving his version of the world turned upside down: *Hen Gerddi Gwleidyddol* (undated)

Since then the anti-christian crew
Be prest and overthrowne,
Wee'l teach the nobles how to crouch,
And keep the gentry downe;
Good manners hath an ill report,
And turnes to pride we see;
Wee'l therefore cry all manners downe,
And hey then up go we.

C An English poet wrote this poem entitled *The Round-heads Race* published in a pamphlet called *The Distractions of Our Times* (1642)

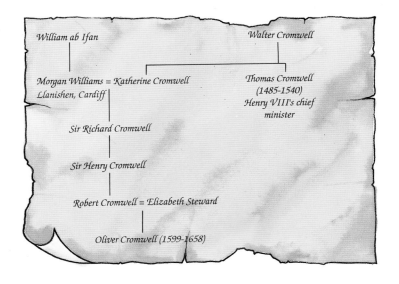

D A family tree showing Oliver Cromwell's Welsh connection.

Eleven years of Republican rule turned the Welsh against Cromwell. Both rich and poor, were ready to welcome back the Stuart monarchy. But as long as Cromwell lived they dared not do anything.

After the death of Cromwell everything changed. In north Wales in 1659, Sir Thomas Myddleton of Chirk Castle rose in revolt. The revolt was crushed by Cromwell's son and Myddleton was briefly imprisoned. In south Wales, at Haverfordwest, tradesmen (cobblers, hatters, weavers and tailors) went on strike. In a Llanddeiniolen alehouse an old Royalist soldier named Lewis Morris declared publicly: 'a turd in the state's teeth … I care not if they and all Roundheads were hanged.' In 1660, by popular demand, Charles II returned and the monarchy was restored.

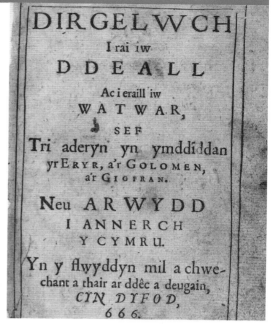

The original title page of Morgan Llwyd's *Llyfr y Tri Aderyn* (Book of the Three Birds)

 E In his book *Llyfr y Tri Aderyn* (Book of the Three Birds) Morgan Llwyd imagines a conversation between three birds, each of whom represents Cromwell (the Eagle), the Royalists (the Raven) and the Puritans (the Dove) (1653)

RAVEN:	They (the Puritans) are a deceitful [untrustworthy] people; they speak fairly, and offer long prayers that [mean] nothing after all.
EAGLE:	Let us ask the Dove to answer for herself. What say you?
DOVE:	It is better to say nothing to unreasonable folk: but the truth is that we meet frequently, that we speak fairly, that we try to do good to everybody, and that we would wish to do better. And if it can be proved that we have [tried] to hurt anyone, take your revenge upon us. And as to the long prayers, you yourself realise that we receive almost everything for which we ask.
EAGLE:	Name one thing that the Doves received.

DOVE:	We prayed that the Doves should [win] the war.
RAVEN:	Were you doves in the war? You were more like devils by far.
DOVE:	It is true that some unruly birds joined our party, and that it was they who did wrong through the lands.
RAVEN:	I have it in my heart to kill this smooth-tongued Dove.
EAGLE:	Enough. I see you wish to start another war if you could. Enough of fighting; you have been defeated too often.
RAVEN:	Maybe, but my day will yet come.

1 a) Which source suggests that the aristocracy and gentry had every reason to fear the rule of men like James Berry? Explain your choice.
   b) Major General James Berry proved to be a fair and successful ruler of Wales so why did the Welsh gentry hate him so much?
   c) Give two reasons why the ordinary Welsh people might also hate him?
   d) What evidence can you find in the text and sources to suggest that Cromwell's attempt to convert the Welsh to Puritanism would end in failure?

2 a) Look at source A. Make a list of the ways in which the artist has shown the world turned upside down.
   b) Read source E. Do you think Morgan Llwyd was a Raven or a Dove? Support your choice with evidence from the source.
   c) Suggest reasons why 'Bird Books' like these may have been popular in Wales during the period of Cromwell's rule.

*W*ales and the Welsh: language, culture and customs

Wales was a conquered country in the 16th century. Her great leaders, men like Prince Llywelyn ap Gruffydd and Owain Glyndwr, had been defeated or killed by the English. The English came in large numbers to settle in Wales. Most English people did not understand the Welsh people or their customs or **culture**. Sometimes this led to bitter disputes between the two peoples.

Henry Tudor's victory at Bosworth changed the relationship between Wales and England. After 1485 large numbers of Welsh people settled in England. Under Henry VIII Wales was united with England. The Welsh people and the English had to learn to live together.

 (left and below) John Caxton, an English printer, describes the Welsh in his book *The Description of Britain* (1480)

The way of life in Wales is very different from that in England in matters of food, drink, dress and in many other aspects. The people are extremely well dressed in a shirt, mantle and an excellent pair of trousers to protect them against the wind and rain. In this garb they brave the weather, even though it is extremely cold. They always go about in this garb; fighting, amusing themselves, leaping, standing, sitting, and even sleeping without sheets all the time ... they are always bare legged. They practise no other way of going about even if they are to meet the King.

The people are capable of going for a long time without food [although] they know how to eat and enjoy themselves. They eat hot and cold barley-bread and oat cakes; these being wide, round thin biscuits. They have a kind of gruel for soup, accompanied by leeks, butter, milk, and cheese. They eat such [foods] eagerly; this causes them to drink mead and strong ale in large quantities; often all day and all night. They tell many idle stories; for when they are occupied with drinking they are full of talk. Both at and after meals they greatly enjoy salt and leeks.

Whether at home or out, they keep their money and their comb suspended from their [trousers]. It is remarkable that they are so fastidious [fussy], detesting farting, when they do not [hesitate] at disposing of their excrement at their very door. At great banquets they have harps, tabors [small drums] and pipes to provide music. They are fond of observing family relationships, even when distant to the hundredth degree!

They set themselves up above others, though they greatly [respect] priests and honour Almighty God's servants like heavenly angels.

The beastly manner of these Celts have now improved by contact with the [English]. They cultivate gardens, fields, and slopes and congregate together in pleasant towns. They ride about fully armed, wearing breeches and shoes. They sit pleasantly at their meals and sleep in many a comfortable bed. To anyone considering them, they seem more like Englishmen than Welshmen nowadays. If people should wish to know the reason, it is because they now live at peace more than they [used] to do.

 Modern sculpture showing the fourteenth-century dress of a Welsh gentleman and poet, Dafydd ap Gwilym

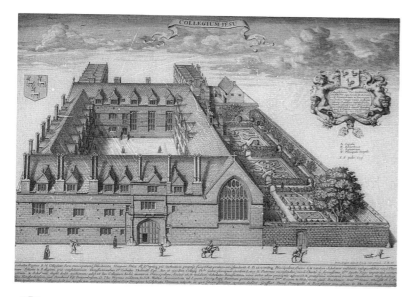

C A contemporary drawing of Jesus College, Oxford. The college was founded in 1571 by Hugh Price of Brecon for Welsh students

Praise God that thou hast careful parents to place thee in Oxford, a famous university, the fountain … of all learning. Keep company with honest students who abhore [hate] evil courses as drinking and taking tobacco … Speak no Welsh to any that can speak English, … and thereby that you should keep company with studious, honest Englishmen than with many of your own countrymen who are more prone to be idle and riotous than the English.

D A letter by William Wynn of Glyn Cywarch, Merionethshire, to his son Cadwaladr at Oxford University (about 1638)

You will find some men that, so soon as they see the river Severn, or the steeples of Shrewsbury, and hear the Englishman but once say 'Good Morrow', they shall begin to put their Welsh out of mind and to speak it in most corrupt fashion. Their Welsh will be of an English cut, and their English (God knows) too much after the Welsh fashion. And this cometh either of very foolishness or of a saucy pride and vanity. For he is never seen for a kindly, [honest] man that will deny … his country or his tounge.

E Gruffydd Robert, a Catholic clergyman and scholar exiled to Italy during Elizabeth's reign wrote a book on Welsh grammar (1567). In the introduction to the book he comments on the spread of English influence in Wales

F Picture of Hugh Price of Brecon, esquire

1 Read source A. Gather information on the following aspects of Wales and the Welsh people:
 a) dress;
 b) food and drink;
 c) entertainment/recreation.
 Now write down your findings under the above headings into your books.

2 Read source A again.
 a) Write down any facts you can find.
 b) Write down any opinions you can find.
 c) Explain how you decided that they were opinions rather than facts.
 d) In your opinion, how reliable is source A?

3 a) Explain how sources D and E support Caxton's opinions of the Welsh.
 b) In your own words explain Gruffydd Robert's criticisms of the Welsh.
 c) How do sources D and E contradict (disagree with) each other?
 d) Do you find anything unusual about William Wynn's advice to his son? Explain your answer.

Language, scholars and books

Wales may have lost her independence, but she did not lose her identity. Keeping a separate Welsh identity depended on the survival of the language. In the sixteenth century over 90 per cent of the people of Wales spoke the Welsh language. The majority of them could speak only Welsh, they did not understand nor could they speak English. Therefore, unlike some of the gentry, the ordinary people continued to enjoy a culture, tradition and language different from their English neighbours.

Although some of the Welsh gentry had adopted English manners, customs and speech, just as many remained thoroughly Welsh. William Herbert, Earl of Pembroke, was a rich and powerful landowner. He, and others like him, were keen **patrons** of their native culture and language. He was a Welsh speaker who always spoke his mother tongue in preference to English. He did this even in the presence of Queen Elizabeth. Fortunately for him, she did not mind. Elizabeth had learnt some Welsh and could perhaps understand what was being said.

This different cultural tradition and language was kept alive by the works of great scholars and talented poets known as the bards. Tudor scholars like Sir John Price, William Salesbury, the Reverend Edmwnd Prys and Bishop Richard Davies wrote or translated books into Welsh. Perhaps the most famous scholar in Elizabethan Wales was Bishop William Morgan. His translation of the Bible into Welsh ensured the survival of the language.

Other scholars produced books on Welsh grammar. The earliest was written by Gruffydd Robert in 1567. He was followed by Siôn Dafydd Rhys in 1592, Henry Salesbury in 1593 and Dr John Davies of Mallwyd in 1621. Welsh-English dictionaries were also produced at this time.

One of the most popular books published in the Welsh language during the Stuart period was *Canwyll Y Cymru* (The Welshman's Candle). Written by vicar Rhys Prichard of Llandovery during the

A Portrait of William Herbert, first Earl of Pembroke (1557)

B The title pages of Sir John Price's *Yny lhyvyr hwnn* (1546/7)

It is fitting that some of the holy scripture be put into Welsh, because there are many Welsh people who can read Welsh but who cannot read one word of English or Latin, especially those matters which are necessary for every Christian to know lest his soul be [put] in peril. I have decided, because of the love I have for my country, to convey these matters to them in Welsh in order to give them a taste for the sweet and pure will of God and for the salvation [safety] of their souls.

C Sir John Price of Brecon (1502-55) published the first printed book in Welsh called *Yny lhyvyr hwnn* (In this Book) in 1546/7. Price was a government official and scholar. He was responsible for the first translation of the Lord's Prayer into Welsh

1640s, the book was intended for the common people of Wales. It contained catchy verses and popular religious stories. It became known as the 'Vicar's book' and was an instant success.

Later scholars turned to publishing books in Welsh on subjects like science, geography and history. In 1716 Theophilus Evans published his popular but biased history of Wales in Welsh, *Drych y Prif Oesoedd* (Mirror of the Chief Ages).

However, by the end of the eighteenth century the Welsh language was in decline. This led to fewer books in Welsh being published. There was little support from the wealthy gentry who had all but deserted their native language and culture. A new generation of scholars had to fight to preserve the Welsh way of life.

G A drawing showing printers at work (1560). The art of printing enabled many more, and cheaper, books to be published than was possible in medieval times. Between 1547 and 1730, nearly 700 books were published in the Welsh language

Though wert the first put in my hand,
When yet I could not understand,
And daily didst my young eyes lead
To letters, till I learnt to read

D Henry Vaughan, a landowner, wrote a poem in praise of the Welsh translation of the Bible (1646)

This book, next to the Bible, was my earliest reading book. I read and re-read its homely rugged rhymes till I could repeat the greater part off by heart. It was my great grandmother's constant companion. In spite of her great age she could read large print without glasses, and the Vicar's Book was seldom out of her hands, except when she was knitting.

E Extract from Robert Roberts's Autobiography (c.1860s). Roberts was an author and cleric and known as *Y Sgolor Mawr* (The Great Scholar)

God help silly people ... an excellent book, they say, is the Vicar's Book, yes by God say I, it is a fine book indeed ... The Lord have mercy upon us, what a stupid stock we are.

F Lewis Morris, a famous poet and scholar from Anglesey had this to say about Vicar Prichard's book (1760s)

---

1 **Which sources are useful for learning about:**
   a) **Why these books were written and translated;**
   b) **What these early Welsh books looked like;**
   c) **How these books were made;**
   d) **Why these books were so popular;**
   e) **How the translation of the Bible and Rhys Prichard's book helped save the Welsh language?**
   Explain your choice in each case.

2 a) **Read source C. Give three reasons why Sir John Price published his book.**
   b) **Read source F. In your opinion, is Lewis Morris praising or criticising Vicar Prichard's book? Explain your answer.**

Poets and *eisteddfodau*

The most respected and influential scholars in Wales were the bards. They were professional poets who could trace their origins back to medieval times. The *Gogynfeirdd* or Poets of the Princes had entertained members of the royal houses of Deheubarth, Gwynedd and Powys in verse and song. After the conquest of Wales and the deaths of the Welsh Princes, the bards found new patrons willing to reward them for their art; the *Uchelwyr* or gentry.

It took seven years of hard training to become a fully qualified bard. Hopeful young poets would serve their apprenticeship in the company of well-known professional bards. They would follow them as they travelled around the country from one gentleman's house to another. In this way they also would become known to the wealthy and powerful gentry patrons of their masters.

The bards were popular because they also entertained the mass of the common people. The arrival of a bard in the village was worthy of great celebration. At a time when few could read, the spoken verse and songs of the bards were considered to be very important. They not only entertained but brought news of the outside world.

The bards had the power to influence the people by spreading new ideas and propaganda. The success of the Glyndŵr rebellion and Henry Tudor's victory at Bosworth owed much to their support. Henry Tudor never forgot the debt he owed his bardic supporters. During his reign the Tudor royal court always celebrated St David's Day. Welsh bards and musicians, especially harpists, would be invited to London to entertain the king.

In France I sat, though cold my heart,
In Spain I saw the armies start.
In Scotland too, I saw them fight,
Hither and yon, a dreadful sight.
Ireland it was that pleased me best
My main complaint, an empty chest.

B Thomas Prys wrote this poem about his experiences as a soldier in Europe (c.1600)

C The Bards were regular visitors to gentry homes such as this one at Beaupre Castle, near Cowbridge

D Portrait of Katheryn of Berain (Denbighshire) (1568). The bards composed many poems in her honour calling her *Mam Cymru* (Mother of Wales)

The bards would often come together in meetings called *eisteddfodau.* Here they would compete against each other for prizes such as the title of *Pencerdd* or Chief of Song. It was also an opportunity for them to meet, to share ideas and to ensure that the standards of their art were being maintained. It was during these *eisteddfodau* that apprentice poets would be examined and then passed or failed.

Local *eisteddfodau* were held fairly regularly but the three most important national events were held at Carmarthen in 1451 and at Caerwys in 1523 and 1568. The second Caerwys *Eisteddfod* was particularly important because it was ordered by Queen Elizabeth herself.

However, times were changing. An attempt to hold another *eisteddfod* at Caerwys in 1594 came to nothing. By the beginning of the seventeenth century the bardic art was in decline. Many of the great bards like Gruffydd Hiraethog, William Llŷn, Simwnt Fychan, William Cynwal and Siôn Tudur were dead. The new generation of poets were not as good and they refused to change their ancient art. Much of their poetry was out of date and the gentry either did not care for the old ways or they had become more English in speech and manners. This upset poets like Edward ap Raff who complained that 'the world has become all English'.

The bards had to wait until 1789 for the next great *eisteddfod*. At this time better educated people were, once again, becoming interested in the old poetic art. This was the beginning of the modern *eisteddfodau* that are so well known to us today.

> *Whereas it has come to [our] knowledge ... that vagrant and idle persons naming themselves minstrels, rhymers and bards are lately grown into such ... multitude within ... North Wales, that not only gentlemen and others [are upset] by their shameless disorders ... But also the expert minstrels and musicians in tongue and cunning [are] thereby much discouraged to travel in the exercise and practice of their knowledge. Knowing you to be men both of wisdom and upright dealing and also of experience and good knowledge in the science, have appointed and authorised you to ... admit [bards] you shall find worthy.*

The Great Glyndwr no longer could contain,
But, like a furious lion, burst the chain,
None could resist his forces: like timorous [timid] deer
The coward English fled, aghast with fear.

F Poems like this one written by Evan Evans reflect this revival in Welsh culture: *The Love of Our Country* (1772)

E An order by the Queen and Privy Council to Sir Richard Bulkeley, Sir Rhys Gruffydd, Ellis Price and William Mostyn, esquires, to organise an *eisteddfod* at Caerwys (1568)

1 a) Give three reasons why the bards were so popular.
   b) Give three examples to show how powerful and influential the bards could be.
   c) Explain why the number of bards and the bardic art was declining in the seventeenth century.

2 Read source E.
   a) Why did Queen Elizabeth order the Caerwys Eisteddfod to be held in 1568? List as many reasons as you can find in the source.
   b) In your opinion, which reason would Elizabeth have considered the most important? Explain why.

3 a) In your opinion, how important a part did the eisteddfod play in ensuring the survival of Welsh culture, tradition and language?
   b) How important a part does the eisteddfod play in the life and culture of Wales today?

16 Restoration and revolution

The Restoration of 1660 meant the return of the monarchy. After the strict rule of the Puritans, the people of Wales and England welcomed Charles II. However, 1660 also saw the return of some old problems; religion and Parliament.

Charles was determined not to lose his head. He was keen to work with Parliament but he refused to be ruled by it. Parliament was divided. Some MPs were suspicious of the king. They formed themselves into a group or party called the **Whigs.** Another group called the **Tories** supported the king.

The king and Parliament could not agree on two main points; money and religion. The king argued that the £1 million he was given every year was not enough to run the country. Parliament refused to increase it.

The king was a Catholic but he practised his religion in secret. He knew his faith would not be popular in a Protestant country. Charles wanted to allow the people to worship as they wished. This would include Catholics, Puritans and any other religious group.

Parliament was less tolerant. It had supported the restoration of the Anglican Church in 1660. Between 1661 and 1665 it passed a series of Acts against these **Nonconformists** - who did not support the Church of England. Charles was angry but did nothing. He knew he could not ignore Parliament so he tried to avoid serious arguments.

The kingdom under Charles II was very different from what it had been under the Puritans. Charles was known as the Merry Monarch because of his cheerfulness and gaiety. He encouraged the return of drama, music and sports, like football.

Charles II's reign is chiefly remembered for two events. The Great Plague of 1665 which killed more than 70,000 people in London and the Great Fire of London in 1666. The fire lasted a week but killed only 20 people.

Who ever here on Sunday
Will practise playing at ball
It may be before Monday
The Devil will have you all.

A Notices like this one put up on the churchyard stile by the churchwardens of Llanfair Discoed in Monmouthshire, were taken down during Charles II's reign

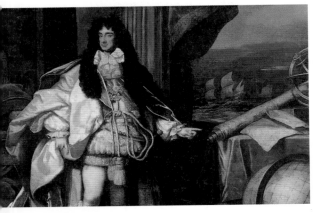

B Contemporary painting of Charles II as patron of the Royal Society

C *(below)* This picture was painted by a Dutch artist who was an eye-witness to the fire

In 1685 Charles II died. He had no children by his wife so he persuaded Parliament to accept his brother James as king. Unlike Charles, James II was not a popular choice. Like his father Charles I, James believed in the Divine Right of Kings. He quarrelled with Parliament and tried to rule without it.

James was also a Catholic but unlike his brother he openly displayed the fact. This upset the people. Within a few months of becoming king there was a rebellion. It was led by the Protestant Duke of Monmouth, one of his brother's 14 **illegitimate** children. It failed.

The rebels were treated harshly, and 250 were executed by the cruel Judge Jeffreys. Known as 'The Hanging Judge', this Welshman from Wrexham showed no mercy. A further 1,000 rebels were transported to the West Indies as slaves.

After three years of being king James had upset just about everybody. He ignored Parliament, had increased the size of his army and promoted Catholic friends to positions of power. Once again a Stuart monarch looked set to cause another revolution. It came in the autumn of 1688.

James's daughter Mary had married William, Prince of Orange and ruler of Holland. Both were Protestants and both were willing to rule with Parliament and not against it. They were invited by Parliament to become joint rulers of the kingdom. William landed in Devon with an army of 15,000 men. James's friends and his army deserted him. He fled to France never to return.

This is known as the Glorious Revolution because no-one was killed; it was bloodless. Parliament was determined this time to get it right. In 1689 they passed a Bill of Rights which said what a king could and could not do. William had no choice but to accept it. From now on, Parliament would have a powerful voice in the government of the kingdom.

D Contemporary portrait of James II

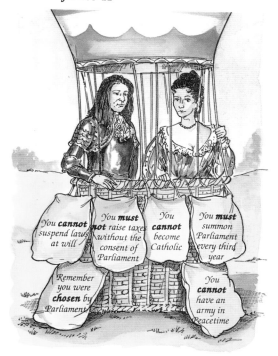

You *cannot* suspend laws at will

You *must not* raise taxes without the consent of Parliament

You *cannot* become Catholic

You *must* summon Parliament every third year

Remember you were **chosen** by Parliament

You *cannot* have an army in peacetime

E (right) How the Bill of Rights restrained William and Mary

1 **Look at sources B and D.**
a) **Why might source B have been painted after 1662? Look ahead to the chapter entitled 'Superstition and Science' to help find the answer.**
b) **Date source D. Explain how you reached your conclusion.**
c) **Compare sources B and D. How have King Charles and King James been portrayed (shown) by the different artists?**
d) **Do you think the decision to paint the two kings in this way was taken by the artist or the monarchs themselves? Explain your answer.**

2 **In your opinion, are pictures and cartoons like those shown in this chapter, more or less useful to an historian than written sources? Explain your answer.**

3 **Read the text and then compare Charles II and his brother James II as kings of England.**
a) **Make a list of the similarities and differences between the two monarchs.**
b) **Name two events for which Charles II's reign will be remembered.**
c) **Now do the same for James II's reign.**
d) **Who, in your opinion, was the more successful king? Give reasons.**

17 *W*omen in early modern Britain

A historian once said that history has been only half written. This is because half the population has been largely ignored; the female half. Even history books like this usually have but one chapter on the history of women. Why?

Much of our history has been written by men about men. They wrote about kings, nobles, wars and politics. They rarely wrote about women unless they were queens like Elizabeth (1558-1603) or Anne (1702-1714). But when they did it was usually to offer their opinions or advice on how women should behave.

Some men even wrote books of instructions to help other men set rules for their wives. Sometimes a bride received similar instructions from her father.

A husband could do as he wished but his wife could not. The law was made by men. In 1603 Parliament passed a new common law which said that women had no legal rights to property or freedom of choice once they were married. They and all their possessions belonged to their husbands.

THE ENGLISH House-Wife,

CONTAINING

The inward and outward Vertues which ought to be in a Compleat Woman.

As her skill in *Physick*, *Chirurgery*, *Cookery*, *Extraction of Oyls*, *Banqueting stuff*, *Ordering of great Feasts*, *Preserving of all sort of Wines*, *conceited Secrets*, *Distillations*, *Perfums*, *Ordering of Wool*, *Hemp*, *Flax* : Making *Cloath* and *Dying* ; The knowledge of *Dayries* : Office of *Malting* ; of *Oats*, their excellent uses in Families : Of *Brewing*, *Baking*, and all other things belonging to an Houshold.

A *Work* generally approved, and now the Ninth time much Augmented , Purged , and made most profitable and necessary for all men, and the general good of this NATION.

By *G. Markham.*

LONDON,
Printed for *Hannah Sawbridge*, at the Sign of the *Bible* on *Ludgate-Hill.* 1683.

A The English House-wife (1673) was one of the most popular books of the time. It was written by a man called Gervase Markham. It gave instructions for men to help them train their brides to be good housewives

B A scold's bridle. This was used to punish gossiping women in the Tudor period

[A husband] must patiently put up with the harshness of his wife, because there is nothing in the world more spiteful than a woman who is annoyed. The husband must not injure his wife by word or deed, for a woman is a feeble creature. She does not have as much noble courage as a man. The husband must make sure his wife is happy … otherwise she will find some place to gossip. But what shall the wife do? …
St Peter speaks to wives like this: 'Let wives be subject to their husbands.' [The wife] must not be jealous or mistrust her husband if he is away.

C Sir William Vaughan of Llangyndeyrn: *The Golden Grove* (1608)

Woman is the weaker vessel, of a frail heart, inconstant, and with a word soon stirred to anger.

D *The Homily on Marriage* (1562). This was part of the church service read on Sundays

A woman must get on with her husband, even if he treats her badly. You must behave yourself, be blind to your husband's faults and work hard at looking after your house and children.

E A letter by Lord Halifax to his daughter (1680)

Even the church held strong views on women. Since all the priests and bishops were men, this is hardly surprising. The teachings of the church were a powerful influence. The Scottish Puritan John Knox, preached against women rulers. His pamphlet, *The First Blast of the Trumpet against the Monstrous Regiment of Women* (1558), upset Elizabeth.

Unfortunately, women did not write about themselves very often. During the Tudor and Stuart period few women could read or write. They were rarely given the opportunity to be educated. They were expected to marry, have children and look after the home.

There were exceptions. Bathsua Makin was a talented scholar particularly in maths and languages. During the reign of Charles II she opened a school for girls and published a book.

Women are of two sorts: some of them are wiser, better learned and more constant than a number of men, but some are foolish, wanton, ... witless, feeble, proud, dainty, tale-bearers ... and in everyway ... the dregs of the devil's dunghill.

 F   Part of Bishop Aylmer's sermon to Queen Elizabeth (1583)

G   The talented wife and the bored husband (1789)

Women ... nature hath made to keep [the] home and to nourish their family and children, and not to meddle with [important] matters ... , nor to [hold] office in a city or [council] any more than children and infants.

H   Extract from Sir Thomas Smith's book, *De Republica Anglorum* (1565)

[Men claim that] women ... have too much tongue ...The tongue is the only weapon women have to defend themselves ... and they need to use it [well, for] if women are fools ... then men can ... make them into slaves.

[Women] should spend their time [being] instructed in those things usually taught to Gentlewomen in schools ... rather than spending time learning to ... dance, to paint their faces, to curl their hair [and] to dress their bodies.

If women were educated I am confident the advantage would be very great ... when women are educated ... they do often equalize, sometimes excel men, in whatever they attempt.

 I   Extracts from Bathsua Makin's, *The Education of Women* (1673)

---

1 Read source C. Does Sir William Vaughan have a good or bad opinion of women? Explain your answer.

2 Read source A.
   a) What were the duties expected of the 'perfect' housewife according to Mr Markham? Use a dictionary to help you to explain difficult words.
   b) What does this source tell us about his attitude to women?

3 Read the text and look at sources B, D, E, F and H.
   a) Which of the sources suggests that the law was made by men and forced on women?
   b) Describe the attitude of the Church towards women in the Tudor period.
   d) Do you think Queen Elizabeth I would have agreed or disagreed with Sir Thomas Smith's view of the role of women? Explain your answer.

4 Read source I.
   a) According to Bathsua Makin why were the majority of women uneducated?
   b) Who does she blame for this?
   c) Do such attitudes to women exist today? Explain your answer.

Superstition and science

A One of the earliest pictures of a witch riding a broomstick appeared in a French book in 1451

B The title page of a book showing Matthew Hopkins examining a suspected witch (1647)

... when suffering from the toothache [you should] eat a mouse 'flayed and beaten' ... the heads of mice burnt, were said to make 'an excellent powder for the scouring and cleansing of teeth called tooth soap'. The blood of an elephant mingled with the ashes of a weasel made a [great] cure for leprosy ... a piece of an elk's hoof, worn in a ring, would keep the owner from the 'falling evil, cramp and fits'.

C Extracts from a sixteenth-century guide to remedies. Quoted in M C Byrne: *Elizabethan Life in Town and Country* (1961)

The people of Wales and England had very simple beliefs. They were taught by the Church to believe in God, the angels and heaven. But they also believed in the devil, witches and hell. People were superstitious. They feared the unknown and the unexplained.

Many believed that evil spirits were responsible for sudden deaths or crops failing. Besides prayers, the people tried magic spells and lucky charms to keep away evil spirits. If these failed they often looked around for someone to blame. Witches were a popular target for hatred and persecution. In most cases they were poor and lonely old women. Their only crime was to look or behave differently.

In 1542 Parliament passed the first of many laws against witchcraft. In 1645 Matthew Hopkins was appointed Witchfinder-General. In two years he executed more than 200 people for witchcraft; many were burned alive. The Church joined in the persecution. It said that women were more likely to become witches because 'evil sprang from Eve in the garden of Eden'.

Between 1500 and 1730 more than 100,000 people were put to death in Europe. The last trial for witchcraft in Britain was in 1722. In 1736 Parliament changed the law and witchcraft ceased to be a crime.

Attitudes were changing. Men were turning to science to provide answers. They carried out experiments to prove their ideas correct. An Italian astronomer Galileo (1564-1642) discovered that the earth moved around the sun. In 1628 an Englishman, Sir William Harvey (1578-1657), proved that the heart pumped blood around the body. This was the most important medical discovery of the century.

D Charles I was so impressed with Harvey's ideas that he was invited to Court to explain them. This is a nineteenth-century artist's impression of the scene

Yet there were some who refused to accept these new ideas. The Church was the most powerful enemy of science. It feared that scientists might turn to questioning the existence of God. This fear caused the Pope to sentence Galileo to seven years in prison for his ideas. Harvey was accused of heresy because he tried to disprove the existence of witches.

However, nothing could stop the progress of science. In 1662 King Charles II agreed to set up the Royal Society to help scientists meet and discuss their ideas. Mathematicians like William Jones of Llanfihangel Tre'r Beirdd in Anglesey and astronomers like Edmund Halley became members. Two of the most famous members of the Society were Robert Boyle (1627-91) and Sir Isaac Newton (1642-1727). Boyle's ideas lay the foundation for modern chemistry. Newton's books, especially *Principia Mathematica*, were responsible for modern physics, mathematics and astronomy. In 1687 Newton's experiments led him to his greatest discovery; **gravity**.

By the eighteenth century, scientific experiment had replaced guesswork in science and medicine. New inventions like the telescope in 1600 and the microscope in 1655 made it possible for scientists to be more accurate in their conclusions.

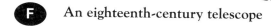

F An eighteenth-century telescope

Mr. Hooke read a ... very curious [interesting] lecture about the late comet, ... proving very probably that this is the very same comet that appeared before, in the year 1618, and that in such a time probably it will appear again - which is a very new opinion. Here was [a] very fine [lecture and] experiments ... but I do lack philosophy [brains] enough to understand them.

E Extract from Samuel Pepys's Diary (1665). Pepys was a government official, the Secretary to the Admiralty

G By using a microscope like the one shown in the photograph, Robert Hooke was able to see what a flea looked like.

---

1 **Read the text and sources then answer the following questions fully.**
   a) **Give two reasons why people believed in witchcraft.**
   b) **When and from where did the idea that witches rode broomsticks come from?**
   c) **Describe the sixteenth-century cures for leprosy, toothache and fits. Were they likely to work?**

2 **What did the following people discover:**
   a) **Galileo;**
   b) **Harvey;**
   c) **Newton?**
   d) **Were the Stuart kings of England for or against the new scientific ideas?**

Give reasons for your answer.
   e) **Find and list the names of the two Welshmen mentioned in the text. Explain how you came to choose them.**

3 **Read source E.**
   a) **What is the name of this comet? (Clue: it is named after a scientist mentioned in the text).**
   b) **Why do you think it was named after this scientist and not Robert Hooke?**

4 **Explain why you think the Church:**
   a) **taught people that witches and other evils existed;**
   b) **opposed the new scientific thinking?**

In Tudor times few children in Wales went to school. This was because there were less than 20 schools and only people like merchants and wealthy landowners could afford to send their children to them. They were called grammar schools because they taught Latin and Greek grammar. Pupils were beaten if they were caught speaking English or Welsh.

The Puritans believed that grammar schools for the rich were wrong. They wanted to teach all children to read the Bible. Between 1650 and 1653 more than 70 free schools were set up in the towns of Wales. These Gospel schools had little success because they taught only reading in English. The majority of Welsh children from the poorer classes could only speak and understand Welsh.

In 1670 Thomas Gouge set up the Welsh Trust. Nearly 300 schools were opened between 1670 and 1681. He believed that children should be taught to write as well as read. Gouge claimed that nearly 1,500 people in 51 Welsh towns had been taught to read the English Bible in the first two years.

The Puritans and the Trust worked hard to educate Welsh children, but failed. They did not see how important the Welsh language was to the people. So the Society for the Promotion of

A An early seventeenth-century Horn book, used for learning to read

B Page from Thomas Jones's copy book (1683). Such books were used to teach people to write

C A painting of Griffith Jones as a young man

Christian Knowledge or SPCK allowed their teachers to teach in Welsh in some schools. The SPCK believed that children should be taught to read, write and do arithmetic. Some of its teachers even fed and clothed the poorer children. Between 1699 and 1717 the SPCK gave away 10,000 Welsh Bibles to pupils it had taught to read in its 180 charity schools. The SPCK came to an end because there was a shortage of good teachers and its leaders quarrelled.

One of the SPCK's most successful teachers was Griffith Jones. He had run a charity school at Laugharne before becoming vicar at Llanddowror near Carmarthen. Griffith Jones was a very religious man. He wanted the people to be good Christians. He believed that adults as well as children should be taught to read the Bible in Welsh. With the help of some wealthy friends, Jones decided to open schools in other parts of Wales.

Jones trained his teachers and then arranged for them to visit Welsh towns and villages. They were paid between £3 and £4 a year. These teachers usually stayed for about three months and then moved on to another area. The schools met in local churches, barns or in any other building that was available. Because they moved around Wales, the schools were known as circulating schools. They were cheap and easy to run.

Griffith Jones relied on the support and charity of rich landowners like Sir John Philipps of Picton Castle and Madam Bridget Bevan of Laugharne. To keep them informed he published an annual report called *Welsh Piety.* According to his reports, 3,500 circulating schools managed to educate nearly 160,000 people between 1736 and 1761. This was a great achievement.

Jones's fame spread far and wide. In 1764 Catherine the Great, Queen of Russia, sent her ministers to learn more about the circulating schools. Soon others were copying his schools.

After Griffith Jones's death in 1761 the circulating schools were run by Madam Bevan. Their continued success was due to her hard work. By the time of her death in 1779, the number of people taught to read had nearly doubled; more than half the population of Wales.

In the second half of the eighteenth century, Wales was one of the few countries in the world where the majority of the population could read.

 D   John Simkin: *Wales in Industrial Britain* (1993) - a school textbook

English charity schools in Wales are as ridiculous [silly] as French charity schools in England.

E   Griffith Jones: *Welsh Piety* (1738)

Neither the poor nor any others, are, at all, to be taught Writing … it is by no means the design [aim] of this … charity, to make them gentlemen, but christians.

 F   Griffith Jones: *Welsh Piety* (1749)

1 **Answer these questions in sentences:**
   a) **Work out the total number of schools that had been set up in Wales between about 1550 and 1717.**
   b) **How many schools did Griffith Jones set up in Wales between 1736 and 1761?**

2 **Look at sources A and B.**
   a) **Give two reasons why the Horn book in source A would have been used in schools run by the SPCK.**
   b) **Would Griffith Jones have used the copy book shown in source B in his schools?**
   Give reasons for your answer.

3 **Read sources D, E and F.**
   a) **What information can you find on pages 72 and 73 to support source D? Copy out the sentences.**
   b) **Explain the meaning of Griffith Jones's statement in source E.**

4 **Write a paragraph describing the main similarities and differences between your school and the schools you have read about in these pages.**

You ask me if I have seen Mr. Jones? Yes; blessed be to God I have seen him, to my great comfort. He is an old soldier of Jesus Christ, O that I may follow him as he has Christ.

 A Griffith Jones influenced English Methodist leaders like George Whitfield and John Wesley. Whitfield wrote this in 1739

When [Rowland] delivered his ... sermons, cries of 'what must I do to be saved?' echoed around the church and churchyard. Members of Rowland's congregation often roared, trembled, wept, sang, clapped their hands, or fell to their knees ... His flocks were dubbed 'the Welsh Jumpers'... others called them 'the Holy Rollers'.

B Geraint Jenkins, a modern historian, describes a typical Methodist meeting, in 'The New Enthusiasts', *The Remaking of Wales in the Eighteenth Century* (1988)

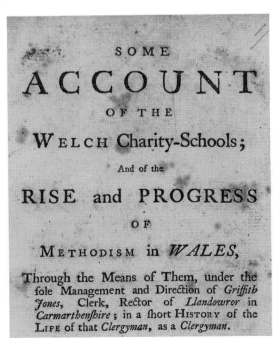

SOME
ACCOUNT
OF THE
WELCH Charity-Schools;
And of the
RISE and PROGRESS
OF
METHODISM in *WALES*,
Through the Means of Them, under the sole Management and Direction of *Griffith Jones*, Clerk, Rector of *Llandowror* in Carmarthenshire; in a short HISTORY of the LIFE of that *Clergyman*, as a *Clergyman*.

C Title page of John Evans's book *Some Account of the Welsh Charity Schools* (1752)

The Methodists revive religion

Although the eighteenth-century Anglican vicar was as important and respected a churchman as the early sixteenth-century Catholic priest had been, there were problems. The people were becoming bored with the Church. Many clergymen were failing to offer the people an exciting and worthwhile religious experience. Some Bishops were lazy and corrupt. Many parish vicars were poor, others were uneducated. In Wales the problems were even greater.

To make matters worse, non-Welsh speaking Englishmen were being appointed to Church livings in Wales. In 1766 the 70-year-old Dr Thomas Bowles was appointed to the parishes of Trefdraeth and Llangwyfan in Anglesey. Of his 500 parishoners only 5 could speak English and so understand his English sermons. The people tried to get rid of him, they even took him to court, but failed.

Some Anglican clergymen were concerned with the depressing state of the Church. They feared there would be a decline in Christian belief. Griffith Jones was one of the first to begin the task of reviving religion. He had intended to become a **missionary** in India but he felt that his own people were so ignorant about religion that he decided to stay in Wales. His great contribution was to bring the word of God to the people by teaching them to read the Welsh Bible.

Griffith Jones was also a fine preacher. He influenced those who heard him to continue his work. Men like Daniel Rowland of Llangeitho, Howell Harris of Trefeca and William Williams of

 D Erasmus Saunders was a caring Welsh vicar who spoke out against the corruption in the Church. Here are some extracts from his report: *A View of the State of Religion in the Diocese of St. David's* (1721)

There is, I believe, no part of the nation more inclined [prepared] to be Religious, and to be delighted with it than the poor Inhabitants of these mountains ... the doctrines [ideas] of the Reformation begun about two hundred years ago in England have not yet effectually reached us.
The poor state of the Church is caused by the [four main] evils of pluralism, ... absenteeism, ... non-residence [and] nepotism.

A good deal of what Saunders had to say was true, but his [criticisms] are [hardly] applicable to the whole of Wales ... the diocese of St. David's was much poorer than ... Bangor and St. Asaph ... We should remember ... that Saunders, resentful and bitter at being refused a bishopric, may well have written in a mood of disillusionment and a fit of pique [irritation].

 E A modern historian's opinion of Saunders's book. Geraint Jenkins: *Literature, Religion and Society in Wales 1660-1730* (1978)

Pantycelyn became famous preachers. They believed that God had called them to their great task of saving the souls of the people. They became known as **Methodists.**

They travelled around much of Wales preaching and teaching. They were young, powerful speakers who spread their great enthusiasm for religion wherever they went. So many hundreds of people turned up to hear Rowland and Harris preach that they often did so in the open air. Their religious meetings were made even more exciting by the hymns written by Williams. Many of them are still great favourites in chapels and churches today.

Not everyone liked the Methodists. Some clergymen refused to allow them to preach in their parishes. Some landowners suspected them of preaching revolution so they broke up their meetings. But no one could ignore or stop them.

F The Methodist Leaders in Wales (undated)

G A cartoon of 1763 showing Methodist preachers as greedy men and their congregations as badly behaved

Wales is a conquered country; it is proper to introduce the English language, and it is the duty of the bishops to promote the English ... language.

H Statement made by Bowles's lawyer in court (1773)

1 Please read source D and the text on page 74.
   a) What was wrong with the Church and religion in England at the beginning of the eighteenth century? List the problems.
   b) According to Erasmus Saunders (source D), the Church and religion in Wales were suffering additional (extra) problems. What were they?
   c) How reliable is Erasmus Saunders's evidence? Explain your answer.
   d) Now read source E. Has this changed your opinion of the value of Erasmus Saunders's evidence? Explain your answer.

2 a) Study the cartoon (source G). Describe what you see. How useful is this source for a historian writing a book on the history of Welsh Methodism? Explain your answer.
   b) By the end of the eighteenth century Methodism had became the largest religious movement in Wales. Is this still true today? Conduct a survey of your class. Make a list of the different religious groups represented. Put the largest group at the top of the list.

The kingdom united

SCOTLAND

Edinburgh

Act of Union
1707

IRELAND

Dublin

Act of Union
1801

Ludlow
ENGLAND

WALES

Act of Union
1536-43

London

B An eighteenth-century drawing showing Oliver Cromwell's attack on the Irish town of Drogheda in 1649. Cromwell massacred men, women and children because the Irish had supported the king in the Civil War

The peoples of Ireland, Scotland and Wales have much in common. They are Celtic peoples related by blood, culture and history. They speak the Celtic languages of Welsh and Gaelic. They also shared a hatred for the English.

Since before the time of William the Conqueror rulers of England had tried to force the rulers of these Celtic countries to submit. Some were very successful. King Henry II invaded Ireland in 1169. King Edward I conquered Wales in 1283. This meant that in 1485 Henry Tudor could be crowned King of England, Prince of Wales and Lord of Ireland. In 1541 Henry VIII was the first English monarch to be crowned King of Ireland.

Only Scotland had kept her independence. When Elizabeth I died in 1603 the Crown went to her cousin King James VI of Scotland. James became the first monarch to rule over a united kingdom. Yet the kingdom was not truly united. Although the Welsh seemed happy to accept union with England, many Scots and Irish were not.

Ireland

The Irish people had never accepted Henry VIII's changes in religion. While England and Wales became Protestant, Ireland remained Catholic. This worried the English. They knew that the Catholic countries of Europe might try to invade the kingdom through Ireland. They were right. Spain attempted to invade during the sixteenth century and France tried in the eighteenth century.

The Irish were thought of as a rebellious people. The most serious Irish rebellion happened in 1689 when James II landed in Ireland to try to reclaim his throne. He got the support of the Irish Parliament.

It took two years and a strong English army under William III to stop the revolt. By 1750 nearly 90 per cent of the land in Ireland was owned by English Protestant settlers. Although these colonists made up only 20 per cent of the population, they were given great power over the Catholic Irish. The English monarchs who sent them there hoped they would keep the native Irish under control. They failed. The colonists and the natives hated each other.

Scotland

Scotland had never been conquered by the English. It kept its Crown and Parliament separate from those of England. Until 1603 that is! Unlike the Irish, the Scots at first seemed happy to join England. It was their Scottish King James who was becoming the ruler of England. But as time went by the Stuart monarchs spent most of their time in London and ignored Scotland.

To make matters worse, the English Parliament came to believe that it was more important than the Parliament in Scotland. Often it did not even bother to ask the Scots their opinion on important matters, like who should rule after the death of Queen Anne who had no children. The English wanted to ask a distant cousin to rule in her place. Because he was a German from Hanover the Scots were not keen. The English were afraid of what the Scottish Parliament might do so they decided to unite the two Parliaments. In 1707 Scottish MPs voted to close their own Parliament in Edinburgh. Most of them had been paid to do this. Many of them were given seats in the Parliament in London.

Those Scots who disagreed with this decision - known as Jacobites - wanted James II's son, James Edward Stuart and his son Charles to rule over them instead of German George. In 1715 they rebelled, but the rebellion failed. In 1745 they rebelled again. Led by Charles Stuart, known as the Young Pretender or Bonnie Prince Charlie, the Scots were savagely crushed. The prince expressed his bitterness at having received no help from Welsh Jacobites when he said, 'I will do as much for my Welsh friends as they have done for me; I will drink their healths'.

The United Kingdom was here to stay.

C A painting of the battle of Culloden in April 1746. The English army (red) massacred the defeated Scottish Jacobites (orange)

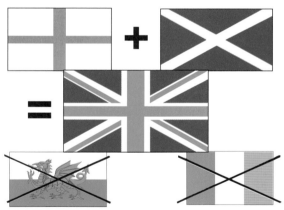

D The making of the Union Flag

1 **a) Write each of these dates on a separate line in your book:** 1169 1283 1485 1536 1541 1603 1707 1801
   Beside each date, write down what events in the story of Britain's unification happened in that year.
   b) Which three dates and their events were the most important in the creation of the United Kingdom? Explain your choice.
   c) Suggest reasons why the Welsh and the Scots were happier to unite with England than the Irish?

2 **a) Which of the three countries was asked to unite with England? Explain why it did so.**
   b) Why were the other two countries forced to unite with England?

3 **a) Look at the map in source A. Write down the names of the capital towns/cities of Wales, England, Scotland and Ireland. Explain why one name should surprise you.**
   b) Look at a map of Ireland today. How has it changed from the one in source A?

21 Change and continuity

Let there be light.
The salt of the earth.
The sign of the times.
The spirit is willing.
The powers that be.

A William Tyndale wanted to change things. He believed that everyone in England should have access to his English Bible even down to 'the boy that driveth the plough'. The English language is crammed with common phrases first given to us by Tyndale

Today we live in an age of great change. It has been said that the world has changed more in the last 95 years of this century than in the whole of the previous 500 years. Why? Developments in science, technology and medicine have greatly affected and altered our lives. There has been a revolution in communications and travel. The pace of life has quickened.

Yet, despite this, even in the twentieth century, some things have stayed the same. This is true of any age. There has always been change but in the early modern world it was not as great or as noticeable as it is today. Or was it?

Religion
Although people still believed in God and continued to attend church, there were great changes in religion which affected almost everyone. The country's official religion changed from being Catholic in 1500 to Protestant by 1600. However, the changes became more complicated. By 1760 the Protestant faith had split into different religious groups. The official Anglican Church was challenged by the Baptists, Independents and the Methodists.

Government
Another change was in the way the country was governed. In 1500 the monarch believed that he governed by 'divine right'. The monarch might still have believed in this idea in 1760, but now he had to share his power with Parliament. During the seventeenth century MPs had begun to question and challenge the power of the monarchy. By the eighteenth century people were no longer willing just to obey, unless they were poor, that is!

B This photograph shows that even in the nineteenth century the living conditions suffered by farm workers in Wales had changed little in 200 years

C Two coins from the seventeenth century

78

The Economy

Some things had not changed. The rich were still rich and the poor were still miserable. In Wales large landowners like Sir John Perrot enjoyed an annual income of more than £1,500. The average Welsh farm labourer could expect little more than £2 a year to live on. The desperately poor had to survive on a lot less. A survey carried out in 1696 by Gregory King suggested that nearly 60 per cent of the population did not earn enough to provide their families with a decent diet.

Society

Some changes would have gone largely unnoticed. The population of England and Wales doubled in size from about 3 million in 1550 to just over 6 million in 1760. **Literacy** (the ability to read and write) was improving.

This was especially true in Wales where the schools of Griffith Jones taught an ever increasing number of people to read. They were lucky enough to have books in Welsh. Men like William Salesbury thought that the Welsh language was doomed. But William Morgan's translation of the Bible changed everything. Although he never intended it to, Morgan's Bible saved the language.

A United Kingdom

Finally, one of the most important changes that occurred during this period was the creation of the United Kingdom. Although the separate identities, cultures and customs of the Welsh, Scots, Irish and English continued to be different, they were moving ever closer to become the British people of today.

(right) **Three paintings of family groups**

1 Look at source C.
   a) Describe the differences between them.
   b) Which coin was issued by King Charles and which was issued by Oliver Cromwell? Explain how you decided.

2 a) Match the paintings (Sources D, E, and F) to the periods and dates (Tudor 1567, Stuart 1645 and Hanoverian 1744) in which these families lived. Explain how you decided.
   b) Describe the changes in fashion which occurred between 1567 and 1744.

3 Make a list of each of:
   a) the changes mentioned in this chapter,
   b) the things that did not change.

4 Write an essay discribing the differences between Wales in 1500 and Wales in 1760. You may find it useful to use the sub-headings used in this chapter.

Glossary

almshouse a house where poor people live, supported by charity
ancestor past family members
ap son of
apprentice a person learning a trade
arable farming by growing crops
assassinate to murder for political reasons
bard professional Welsh poet and minstrel
burgess a townsman
civilisation a well-ordered society
civil war a war between two groups of people in the same country
colonists people who leave one country to settle in another
commerce trade in goods
commonwealth for the good of all in the community
contemporary something or someone from the same period of time
coronation the crowning of a monarch
courtier nobleman living in or around the royal court
culture customs, language, music, poetry and literature of a country
democracy freedom to vote in an election
devout deeply religious
Divine Right monarch's rule by right of God
doublet a close-fitting Tudor garment
economy buying and selling
eisteddfod Welsh festival of poetry, literature and music
empire rule of many lands by one country
enclosure to enclose land with hedges
excommunicate to be thrown out of the Church and refused entry to heaven on death
exile to be sent away
famine failure of crops leading to starvation
gentry class of rich landowners just below the nobility in society
gospel story of the life of Jesus Christ
gravity force causing objects to fall
guild an union to protect the rights and skills of craftsmen
Hanoverian royal family of Britain (from

Hanover in Germany) which ruled from 1714 to 1837
heresy to sin against the Church
heretic person whose religious beliefs are against Church teachings
heir person who inherits after the death of a parent or relative
homily a religious sermon
husbandry farming by rearing livestock
illegitimate person born out of marriage
inhabitant person living in a certain place
intercept to catch something on its way from one person to another
Interregnum period of rule by Puritans
Jacobite supporter of James Stuart and his son 'Bonnie Prince Charlie'
jousting sporting combat between knights
JP official appointed by government to keep law and order and to try offences in smaller courts
licence a paper allowing the holder to do something eg. to beg or to sell
literacy ability to read and write
livestock farm animals eg. cows and pigs
martyr a person who dies for a belief
massacre to murder many people
mercenary person who fights for money
Methodist a form of christian religion, which became popular in the 18th century
missionary a preacher who spreads a religion
monarch a king or queen
mutiny a rebellion by sailors or soldiers
navigation the method of planning a route on a map
nepotism giving a job to a family member
nonconformist person(s) who refuses to obey certain rules
pastoral farming by rearing animals
patron person who supports another with money or influence
persecution to destroy those who don't conform
piety deep belief in God

pluralism to hold more than one job
privateer ships licensed to steal from others
propaganda information spread about to persuade people to believe in ideas
prophecy a vision of the future
Protestant a protester against the Catholic Church and the Pope
purify to clean out or get rid of
Puritan a strict Protestant who wants to simplify forms of worship
Quarter Sessions local courts run by JPs
rebellion a fight against a king, ruler or government by the people
reformation to reform or change something
religious houses name given to all monasteries and nunneries
remonstrance to strongly complain
republic the government or rule of a country without a monarch
revolution massive, sometimes violent, change
scriptures religious books and writings
sheriff appointed to keep law and order
Stuart royal family of Britain (from Scotland) who ruled from 1603 to 1714
tilt jousting
Tories political party set up in the late 17th century to support the Stuart monarchy - later to oppose the Hanoverian monarchy
transcript an accurate copy of an original document
treason when a person betrays their country or monarch
Tudor royal family of Britain (from Wales) who ruled from 1485 to 1603
urban a built up area, larger than a village
vagrant a poor person who wanders the countryside in search of work or food
Whigs political party set up in the late 17th century to oppose the Stuart monarchy - later to support the Hanoverians
yeoman class of small landowner below the gentry in society

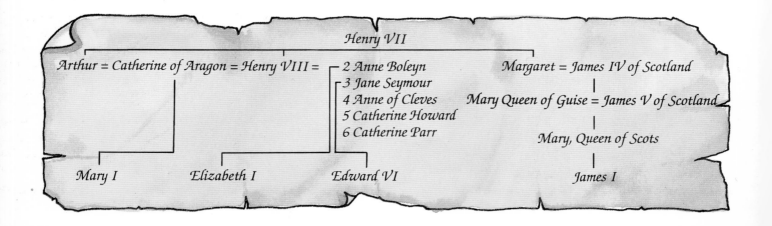

Henry VII

Arthur = Catherine of Aragon = Henry VIII = 2 Anne Boleyn   Margaret = James IV of Scotland
3 Jane Seymour
4 Anne of Cleves   Mary Queen of Guise = James V of Scotland
5 Catherine Howard
6 Catherine Parr

Mary, Queen of Scots

Mary I   Elizabeth I   Edward VI   James I